CHRISTIAN SCHOOLS INTERNATIONAL
3350 East Paris Ave., SE
P.O. Box 8709
Grand Rapids, Michigan 49508

ISBN 0-87463-573-X

Contents

Acknowledgments 5

Introduction 7

Chapter 1 Pond Communities 9

Chapter 2 Sound 33

Chapter 3 Food Plants 45

Chapter 4 Bones and Muscles 59

Chapter 5 Weather 75

Chapter 6 The Oceans 95

Chapter 7 Machines and Work 107

Chapter 8 Packages 121

Supplementary Material 133

Glossary 139

Acknowledgments

Rick Klooster wrote the four books in this science series for grades 3-6 during 1984 and 1985, basing some of the material on a series of science booklets published by Christian Schools International from 1976-82. Mr. Klooster has a bachelor's degree from Grand Valley State College, Allendale, Michigan, and an M.A.T. degree from Calvin College, Grand Rapids, Michigan. He taught in the elementary grades at London Parental Christian School, London, Ontario, from 1975-82, serving as the school's principal during the last four of those years. In 1985 he began teaching at Lafayette Christian School, Lafayette, Indiana.

Serving as consultants to this project were Dr. Uko Zylstra and Dr. John Beebe, both of the biology department of Calvin College. In addition, Dick Oostenink and Kenneth Bergwerff, both of Sylvan Christian School in Grand Rapids, provided a number of the student activities.

Dr. Gordon L. Bordewyk directed the project and served as general editor. Judy Bandstra supervised the production process. The books were designed by Beth Van Rees. Most of the line drawings were created by Joy Visser.

The development of the science series was made possible with grants from Christian Schools International Foundation and Canadian Christian Education Foundation, Inc.

AT & T, 38; American Motors Corporation, 106; Paul Buddle, 32, 41; Burndy Library, 48, 24; Coca-Cola Company, 120; Cousteau Society, 100; Cindy deJong, 37; Edwin deJong, 11, 23, 46, 47, 52, 94, 96, 109, 126, 127; Maynard Juell, 24; Armand Merizon, 102; Michigan Dept. of Agriculture, 12; Michigan Dept. of Natural Resources, 17, 35, 129; National Oceanic and Atmospheric Adm., 74, 83, 89, 90; Texaco, 101; Trane Company, 110; Randall Van Dragt, 19; Judy Zylstra, 8, 29, 33, 34, 36, 40, 45, 46, 48, 51, 53, 61, 64, 71, 78, 111, 113, 114, 116, 122, 123, 124, 130. Cover photo by Edwin deJong.

Introduction

Science is the study of God's world. God's creation is interesting and beautiful. It is also a world of orderliness. The world follows the rules God made for it.

When we study creation, we begin to learn about how the world was made and how it works. We learn God's rules for his world. Studying science can help Christians learn three important things.

First, we learn about God. God created and controls the world. He tells us about himself in his world. The world teaches us how wonderful and how powerful God is.

Second, when we study creation we learn about ourselves. We are part of God's creation—a very special part. God created people to be his workers in the world. God wants us to take care of his creation.

Third, we learn how to care for the world. As God's workers, we need to understand how the creation works. Learning about the living creatures God made can help us take better care of them. Learning about the materials in God's world can help us use them wisely. Learning about the earth can help us care for it and keep from wasting or spoiling it.

As you study God's world in this science book, remember to praise God for his greatness. Learn about how God's world works. And begin to find ways to do God's work in the world.

Chapter 1
Pond Communities

What is an organism?
How do pond animals depend on each other?
How can a microscope help you study pond life?

Have you ever explored a pond? While you were there, did you see frogs, water insects, fish, plants, and other living things?

An **organism** is any living thing. Animals, plants, fish, birds, insects, and even people, are organisms. Every organism lives in a habitat. A **habitat** is the area in which an organism normally lives.

organism (ôr´ gə niz´ əm) any living thing
habitat (hab´ i tat) area in which an organism normally lives

The pond habitat is home to many different organisms. The organisms which live in and around ponds are suited to their habitat. Fish need the water of the pond to live in. Ducks feed on the plants which grow in the pond. Mosquitoes lay their eggs in the pond water. Frogs use the water to escape from their enemies.

Together the different organisms living in the pond area form a **community**. A community is the groups of organisms living in a specific area. The members of the pond community need the pond and each other. God created a balance and order in the pond community. What affects one member of the community can affect other members of the community. As you study this chapter, consider

community (kə myōō´ ni tē) the groups of organisms living in a specific area

how the parts of the pond community work together and how the members of the community need each other.

Focus on the Bible

Pond communities are not accidents of nature. They are part of God's plan. God created pond habitats to be homes for certain kinds of organisms. And he created certain organisms with the abilities to live in pond habitats.

When creating the world, God said, " 'Let the water teem with living creatures, and let birds fly above the earth across the expanse of the sky.' So God created the great creatures of the sea and every living and moving thing with which the water teems, according to their kinds, and every winged bird according to its kind. And God saw that it was good " (Gen. 1:20-21). God created the organisms of the pond community. He wanted the ponds to be full of life.

When we study pond communities we learn about God's creation. We can also learn about God. What can pond communities teach us about God and his creation?

Classifying

classify (**klas** ´ ə fī) sort into groups by characteristics

Classifying is an important skill we use when we study God's world. To **classify** means to sort objects into groups by their characteristics. When we study pond communities, we can classify the organisms which live there based on their characteristics.

Exploring a Pond Community

Take a field trip to a nearby pond community. Be as quiet as you can. Observe carefully, using your senses. Try to learn as much about the pond community as you can.

1. Find a spot near the edge of the pond where you can sit quietly. Look closely. What organisms can you see along the water's edge? What organisms can you spot in the water? Listen to the sounds of the pond community. What is making the sounds?
2. Move quietly to the edge of the pond. Do you see any organisms moving in the water? Are there plants growing in the pond?
3. Different organisms live in different parts of the pond. Some live near the edge of the pond. Others live on the water's suface. Others live beneath the water, along the water's edge, or on the bottom of the pond. Which organisms live where? How many different organisms can you observe?

Compare your observations with those of your classmates.

Characteristics are things you learn about an object or organism by observing. Look at the sketches. Characteristics of **A** are: two-legged, winged, and feathered. **B** is six- legged, winged, and small. Name some characteristics of **C**.

 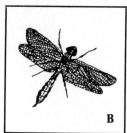 

If you can name characteristics, you can classify objects. Study these groups of organisms. What are some characteristics of each group?

Group 1   Group 2   Group 3

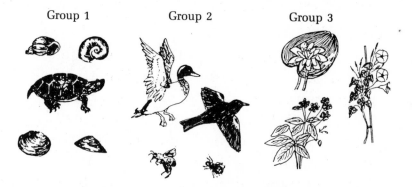

Focus on Biologists

Biologists are scientists who study living things. Biologists study plants and animals. They study how they grow, what they need to live, and many other things.

Biologists use many classification systems in their work. Biologists have divided all living things into two groups: the plant kingdom and the animal kingdom. Within the animal kingdom, large groups, like insects or fish, are grouped together. Still smaller groups, like the group called dogs, are named species.

Every animal and plant is put with the other living things which have similar characteristics. This classification system helps biologists organize and describe living things.

Classifying

Can you classify the students in your room? Try it, using these steps.

1. Divide the students into two groups: light-colored hair and dark-colored hair.
2. Divide each of these two groups according to eye color: brown, blue, and green.
3. Divide each of these six groups into groups of boys and girls. You should now have 12 groups.
4. Copy the classification key. Fill in the names of the students in each group.

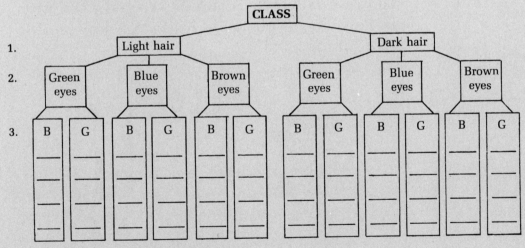

5. Is each group the same size? Do all of the classifications have at least one student in them?

Plants

Plants are a very important part of the pond community. Plants use energy from the sun to produce food energy. Green plants take material from the water and carbon dioxide from the air. They use sunlight to convert these into a sugar (chlorophyll), their food. As plants make food they give off oxygen, a gas that all animals need to breathe.

Plants use the food they produce to live and to grow. They also store some of this food. When an animal eats a plant, that animal gets energy from the plant food. Then the animal uses the energy to live and to grow.

So, green plants provide both food and oxygen to a pond community. Without plants, a pond community would not survive long.

Before reaching a pond, the first plants you probably see are the ones growing on the shore. Willow and aspen trees are common shore plants. They grow best where there is a lot of water. Trees provide shade for the pond. Their roots keep the soil from washing into the pond. The leaves that drop into the pond fill the pond up.

Aspen

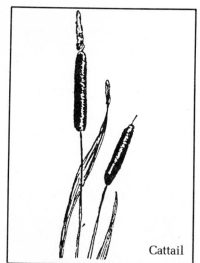

Cattail

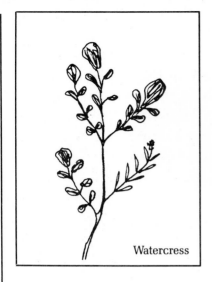

Watercress

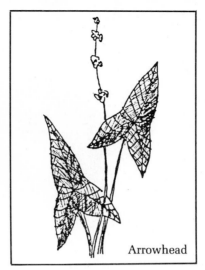

Arrowhead

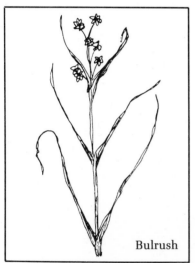

Bulrush

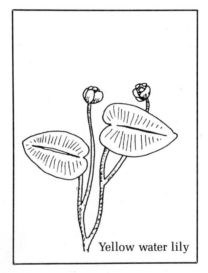

Yellow water lily

At the edge of the pond other plants grow. Cattails are the most common, but watercress, arrowhead, and bulrushes are also found here. These plants may grow at the water's edge or just into the water. They provide hiding places for many small organisms. If you look closely, you may see frogs and minnows hiding among shoreline plants.

Other plants are found farther out into the pond. Some, like water lilies, send their roots into the pond's bottom. Their leaves and flowers float on the surface of the water.

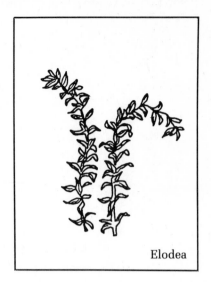

Elodea

Pondweed

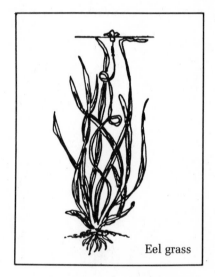

Eel grass

Other plants live beneath the surface of the pond. Elodea is a very common pond plant. Like pond weed and eel grass, elodea is rooted in the pond's bottom. Algae drifts beneath the surface of the pond. It does not have roots. This tiny plant grows in great numbers. It can make the pond water look green. Tiny organisms feed on algae. All the plants which grow beneath the surface of the pond supply oxygen to the organisms of the pond.

Pond Animals and Birds

The animals and birds that live in pond communities vary from one area to another. This chapter describes some of the most common animals and birds. Like plants, they live in different parts of the pond habitat.

Raccoons often visit the pond. You probably won't see a raccoon though, because they come at night to hunt. See if you can find some raccoon tracks.

Crayfish are one of a raccoon's favorite foods. Crayfish often live in holes that are as big around as a quarter. The holes are underwater, close to the shore. Look for them. Do you think this would be a good place to find raccoon tracks?

Kingfisher

Red-winged blackbird

Osprey

Many birds also find food at the pond. Kingfishers and osprey fish in the waters of the pond. Red-winged blackbirds build their nests in the cattails or bulrushes at the water's edge. Blackbirds eat insects they catch near the pond. Ducks and herons also make their nests near the water's edge. Ducks eat duckweed and other pond plants. Herons are fish eaters. They wade in the pond on their long legs and catch fish with their sharp bills.

Duck

Heron

Turtle

Some animals spend most of their lives in the water but can also move around on the land. Turtles spend much of their lives in the pond. Most turtles eat insects and minnows. Snapping turtles eat larger fish and animals. A large snapping turtle can even catch and eat a duck.

Frogs live in the shallow parts of the pond among the weeds and lilies. Frog eggs hatch into tadpoles. Tadpoles eat algae. As the tadpoles grow, they lose their tails and grow legs. They change into frogs. This change is very slow. It takes over a year for a tadpole to change into a bullfrog. Adult frogs eat mostly insects.

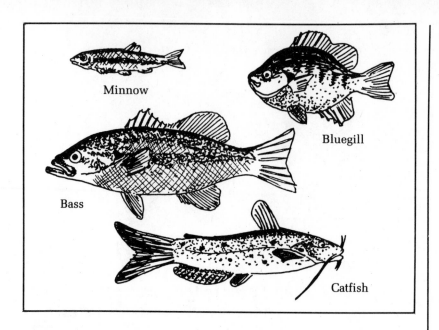

Minnow

Bluegill

Bass

Catfish

Fish are organisms which live entirely in the water of the pond. Many kinds of fish live in pond communities. Minnows, bluegills, perch, bass, and catfish are common pond fish. Generally, small fish, like minnows, eat algae and tiny organisms, while larger fish, like bass, eat smaller fish and insects.

Some insects spend just part of their lives in the water of the pond. During part of their life cycles they are members of the pond community. Some of these organisms are called nymphs when they are young. A **nymph** is a young insect which looks like the adult. Other young organisms are called larvae.

nymph (nimf) a young insect which looks like the adult

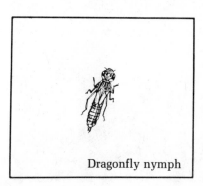

Dragonfly nymph

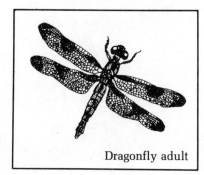

Dragonfly adult

A **larva** does not look like the adult. Both larva and nymphs live in the pond. When they become adults they leave the water.

Young mayflies, damselflies, and dragonflies are all nymphs. As they feed and grow, their wings become larger and stronger. Finally, they leave the water of the pond and fly above it.

Young mosquitoes are larvae. Mosquitoes lay their eggs in the pond. The eggs hatch into mosquito larvae. The larvae eat algae. After awhile the larva breaks open and out comes an adult mosquito. It leaves the pond and flies into the air.

larva (lär ´ və) a young insect which does not look like the adult

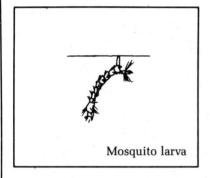

Mosquito larva

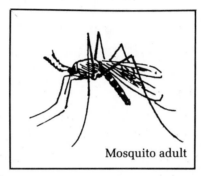

Mosquito adult

Several interesting insects live on the surface of the pond. Water striders walk on water with their long legs. The backswimmer, water boatman, and whirligig beetle swim on the surface of the pond. The whirligig beetle is small and moves around very quickly.

Notice how the legs of these insects are special. God has given them legs which they can use as oars to move around on the pond.

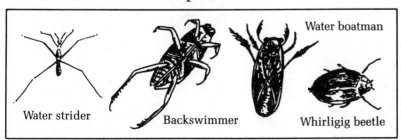

Water boatman

Water strider

Backswimmer

Whirligig beetle

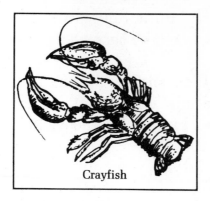
Crayfish

Clam

Snail

In addition to insects, animals, and birds, three other organisms are often found in pond communities. They are crayfish, clams, and snails. The crayfish can be found on the bottom of the pond, often hiding under rocks. Crayfish like to eat minnows and tadpoles. Fresh-water clams can also be found on the pond bottom. Clam shells are easier to find than living clams. Snails also live in the pond. Snails feed on plants and dead organisms. They help keep the pond clean. They also help break up dead organisms into materials which with further decay can be used as natural fertilizer by the plants. Plants need these minerals to grow.

Here are just a few of the other organisms you might find in pond water.

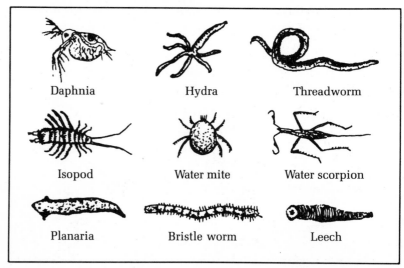

Daphnia   Hydra   Threadworm

Isopod   Water mite   Water scorpion

Planaria   Bristle worm   Leech

Observing a Pond Organism

hand lens (magnifier)
small jar or tray
pond organisms
a net or scoop

What are some of the small organisms that live in a pond? See if you can identify some of the smallest pond organisms.

1. Visit a pond, and scoop some small organisms into a small jar or tray with some water. The organisms will be easier to observe when they cannot move around too much.
2. Study the organisms under your magnifier. Observe how they move. Study what they do.
3. Copy the chart below. Fill in the information for each of the organisms you have found. You might want to make a sketch of some of the organisms.

Name:				
Size:				
Body parts:				
Movement:				
Where found:				
Other:				

Using a Microscope

pond water
microscope
eye dropper
2 microscope slides

A microscope helps you observe organisms which are too small to see clearly with your eyes alone.

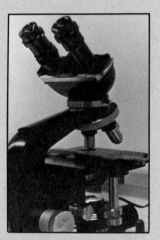

1. Use an eye dropper to place a small drop of pond water on a microscope slide. Cover the slide with a cover slip or another slide. Put it into your microscope.
2. Adjust the microscope until the light in the lens is bright.
3. Adjust the eyepiece until you can see things in the water. Do you see anything moving? If not, make new slides until you see movement.
4. What do you see? How many different kinds of organisms can you find? Draw sketches of some of the organisms you see in the pond water.

Focus on Anton van Leeuwenhoek

The microscope is an important tool. Scientists use microscopes to study many things which cannot be seen with the eye alone.

Anton van Leeuwenhoek helped give science this important tool. He was born in Holland in 1632. Van Leeuwenhoek was not a scientist, but he enjoyed working with lenses. He invented a tool he called the Microscopia. This tool had a small lens, an object holder, and a handle. The object being viewed could be moved closer to the lens until it was in focus. With it, he studied the sting of a bee, the structure of mold, and the parts of blood. He measured the size of the things he saw, and made careful drawings of them.

Today, scientists use much more powerful and accurate microscopes to study the small parts of God's world.

Food Chains

The organisms of the pond community need each other. Plants supply food and oxygen for the other members of the community. Small organisms are food for larger organisms. The larger organisms control the number of small organisms by eating them. The number of organisms at the top of the food chain is controlled by the amount of food available. When there is not enough food, the larger organisms starve. God created the pond community to have balance and order.

We can see this by looking at the pond food chains. Study the food chains shown here. What does each organism eat? How is each organism provided for?

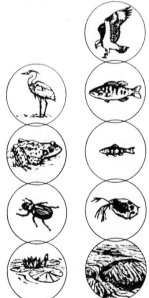

In the pond community, all the food chains are linked together. Many organisms eat more than one kind of food. Most organisms are food for more than one kind of organism. The food chains of the pond are linked together in a food web. A food web is the combination of all the food chains in the community.

What Do Plants Eat?

2 jars
water
water plants
(elodea needs cool, clear water)

Now you know that plants are important in the food chain. How do pond plants grow?

1. Fill 2 jars with water. Place a water plant in each jar.
2. Put one jar in a place with lots of sunlight, like a window ledge. Be careful to keep the water from heating up too much or the elodea will die. Put the other jar in a dark place, like a closet.
3. Check the jars each day, and add water if the water level goes down.
4. After one week study the plants in each jar. How healthy are they? What do the plants need in order to stay alive?

Pond Stewardship

There is a constant cycle of birth and death in the pond. Some animals leave the pond or die. Others move in. Plants grow and die, too. The pond itself also changes. Over many years, a pond grows old and dies. When a habitat changes in an orderly way, we call the changes **succession**.

Ponds form when water fills in a pocket of land. Over many years the pond becomes very different. As the pond goes through the process of succession, both the habitat and the organisms in the community change.

A young pond has only a thin layer of material on the bottom. After a while, sand and humus (decomposing plants, including leaves from the trees nearby) begin to wash into the pond. Slowly the

succession (sək sesh´ ən) orderly changes in a habitat

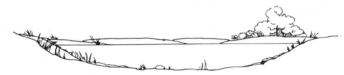

pond begins to fill in. Plants begin to grow in the soil at the edges of the pond. As they die, more humus is added to the bottom of the pond.

The pond becomes smaller and shallower. As pond animals die, their remains are added to the

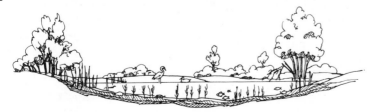

bottom of the pond. So the pond becomes still narrower and shallower. If this goes on long enough, the pond may become a marsh with plants growing completely over it. Finally, it may even become solid land—a field or meadow. After that, it might become a forest.

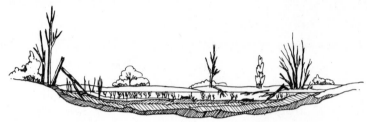

Succession is the natural process of aging which God planned for the pond. People sometimes change the natural process of succession. Sometimes they don't even know they are changing it.

When people dump garbage into the pond, it ages faster, filling up with garbage. If a farmer cuts down trees near a pond, it might also age more quickly or more slowly because of fewer leaves. The tree roots can no longer hold the soil, so it will wash into the pond more quickly.

If the farmer puts fertilizer on crops or a homeowner puts fertilizer on a lawn, the fertilizer may wash into the pond. This might make the pond plants grow too fast. When algae is not controlled by the organisms which eat it, it grows too fast. If algae covers the surface of the pond, the organisms beneath the surface cannot get the air and sunlight they need. Everything except bacteria and blue-green algae in the pond can die if this happens.

Sometimes people fill in the pond with dirt so they can build houses on the land. Sometimes they hunt the birds and animals which live in and around the pond. Sometimes people cut the weeds and plants from the pond so they can swim there.

These changes may change the balance of the community. There may not be enough food, or there may not be enough large organisms to control the number of small organisms.

But not all changes that people make are bad. When people understand how pond communities work, they can make changes which help the pond. For example, a new pond can replace one that people have filled in. A new pond can be made by putting a dam in a stream. A pond will form behind the dam. This pond may become a new home for pond organisms.

Focus on DDT

For years farmers used a chemical called DDT to kill insects. At first it did a very good job of killing insects. Then DDT resistant insects increased. More DDT was used with less effect on the insects but more on the birds. After awhile, people began to notice that there were not as many birds in areas where DDT was used.

Scientists discovered that DDT on the ground can wash into streams and ponds. It gets into the food chain. Small organisms have a little DDT in their bodies. The animals which eat the small organisms have more because they eat lots of little organisms. Large fish had quite a bit of DDT in their bodies. Birds like the osprey and kingfisher which eat fish had the most DDT.

Scientists also discovered that DDT makes birds' eggs very thin. The eggs were breaking before they could hatch. That is why there were fewer birds.

Today people are not allowed to use DDT to control insects. Slowly, over many years, DDT is leaving the food chain. And more birds are in these areas because their egg shells are thicker again.

Review

Summary

The pond is a habitat in which many kinds of plants and animals live. These organisms need the pond to live. They also need each other. Plants supply food and oxygen to the pond community. Small organisms are food for larger animals. The large organisms control the number of small organisms in the pond. The pond ages naturally in God's plan. People affect the pond habitat and community in many ways.

Vocabulary

larva
nymph
community
classify

succession
organism
habitat

Review Questions

1. Name some organisms found in pond communities.
2. In which parts of the pond do different organisms live?
3. Explain pond succession.
4. What are some of the ways people change and destroy pond habitats?

Chapter 2

Sound

How are sounds made?
What is vibration?
What is noise?

Sound is a wonderful gift from God. Sound makes it possible for us to talk to other people. Musical sounds give us pleasure. Warning sounds help us avoid dangers.

Think about the sounds you have heard today. How many can you list? We hear so many different sounds that you probably cannot remember all the sounds you hear in one day.

Making Sound

Sound is a form of energy you can hear. Sounds can be loud or soft, high or low, pleasant or painful. There are many kinds of sound in your world.

All sounds are made by moving objects. When an object moves back and forth quickly, a sound is produced. Back and forth movement is called **vibration**. Vibrating objects produce sound.

Place your hand on your throat, and hum a tune. Can you feel the vibration? Muscles in your throat are vibrating rapidly. This vibration produces a humming sound. When you hear a sound, you know that something is vibrating.

The air is made of many tiny particles. When an object vibrates, it bumps into the air particles around it. The vibration pushes the air particles.

sound a form of energy you can hear

vibration (vī brā´ shən) rapid back and forth movement

33

The air particles closest to the object push other particles. As these particles move, they push still other particles.

The result of all this movement is somewhat like what happens when you drop a stone in water. The stone pushes the water away and waves are formed. The waves move out and away from the stone. Air particles move the same way. In fact, we call the movement sound waves. When an object vibrates, it forms sound waves which move out and away from the vibrating object.

Focus on Bats

God has given bats a special ability which helps them fly at night. Bats cannot see in the dark. Instead, they use sound to find their way.

When a bat flies, it makes a high squeaky sound. The sound waves move away from the bat through the air. When the sound waves hit an object, the waves bounce off the object and travel back towards the bat. The bat listens for the sound waves coming back to it. The direction of the sound andd how long it takes the sound to return help the bat tell where objects are.

Bats are very good at using sound to locate objects.

When scientists put a bat into a room full of thin wires, the bat is able to fly around the room without touching any of the wires. Because of this highly developed sense of sound, bats can fly even when it is too dark for other animals to see them.

Loud and Soft

Not all sounds are the same. Some sounds are very loud, but others are quite soft.

You can see the difference between loud and soft sounds when you pluck a rubber band. Stretch a rubber band between your hands. Pluck it gently. Listen and watch. Is the sound loud or soft? Does the band move far or just a little? Now pluck the rubber band hard. Is the sound louder? Does the rubber band move back and forth farther?

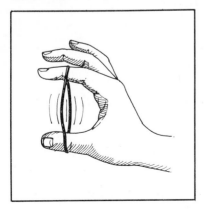 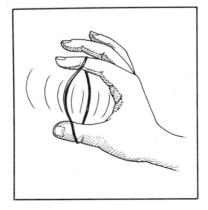

resonance (rez´ ə nəns)
reinforcement of sound by vibration in a second object

Sounds can also be made louder by using resonance. **Resonance** is reinforcement of a sound by vibration or reflection in another object. A sound's vibrations may cause the second object to vibrate. These extra vibrations cause more air particles to move. The sound is made louder.

You can see how resonance works. Place your hands on your cheeks and hum. Can you feel your cheeks vibrating? The spaces in your mouth and nose provide resonance for your voice. Your voice is louder and carries farther because of resonance.

Many musical instruments use resonance. A violin or guitar string does not make a very loud sound by itself. But the violin or guitar body vibrates when the string vibrates. The instrument's resonance makes the string's sound louder.

Producing Resonance

rubber band
paper cup or small box

Resonance makes sounds louder and fuller. Here's a simple activity to show how resonance works.

1. Stretch a rubber band in your hands. Pluck it to make a sound. How loud is the sound?
2. Now stretch the same rubber band around a cup or box. Pluck it again.
3. What is the difference between the two sounds? How do the vibrations create resonance?

Resonance in a Piano

piano
chair to stand on

Did you ever wonder how a piano makes sound? Try to find out.

1. Open up the piano lid so you can see the strings.
2. Play one note and keep the key pressed down.
3. Which strings vibrate? Why do other strings vibrate?
4. Try it with another key. Do the same strings vibrate?
5. Now play three or four notes together. Why is the sound louder when you play more notes?

High and Low

Sounds are not only loud or soft; they can also be high or low. We use the word pitch to describe how high or low a sound is. The **pitch** of a sound is determined by the speed with which the object

pitch (pich) the quality of a sound that makes it seem high or low

vibrates. Fast vibrations make high pitches. Slow vibrations produce low pitches.

The speed with which an object vibrates is its **frequency**. Objects which vibrate at a low frequency—a slow speed—have a low pitch. Objects which vibrate at high frequency—high speed—have a high pitch.

The frequency at which an object vibrates depends on several things. Frequency is related to the length of the object, the tightness of the object, and the material of which the object is made.

Long objects have lower pitches than shorter objects. Take two pieces of string, one long and one short. Pluck them both. Which has the higher pitch? Look at the inside of a piano. Which strings are longest?

When an object is stretched tighter, its pitch is made higher. Take a rubber band. Stretch it a little, then pluck it. Now stretch it tighter. Pluck it again. When the rubber band is stretched tighter, its pitch is made higher.

Objects of the same size but of different materials can also have different pitches. For example, a cotton string and a rubber band, both six centimeters long, will have different pitches.

Focus on Alexander Graham Bell

Alexander Graham Bell was an inventor who made a big difference in the world. He invented the telephone.

Bell was born in England but moved to Canada as a boy. Later, he moved to the United States, but he returned to Canada when he grew older.

Alexander Bell's father wrote books about speech and taught speech to deaf people. Like his father,

Alexander taught deaf children and studied how sounds were made. Bell's study of how people make sounds, and his study of using electricity to produce sounds led to the invention of the telephone in 1876. He once said that he would rather be remembered for teaching the deaf than for inventing the telephone.

Someday, you may be able to visit Bell's house in Brantford, Ontario, or the Alexander Graham Bell Museum in Baddeck, Nova Scotia.

Focus on Ears

You use your ears to hear sounds. Sound waves which travel through the air reach your ear. The sound waves make your eardrum vibrate. The vibrations are transferred from your eardrum to tiny bones in your ear. Tiny hair-like structures in the ear move with the vibrations. These hair-like structures are connected to nerve endings which send messages about the sounds to your brain.

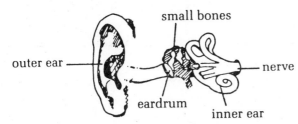

Not all vibrations make sounds which you can hear. Your eardrum only vibrates for a certain range of sound waves. Vibrations which are too fast or too slow do not make your eardrum vibrate.

Some animals can hear higher frequency vibrations than people can. For example, dogs can hear high frequency sounds. A dog whistle makes a sound so high that people cannot hear it but dogs can.

Noise

Our ability to hear sounds is a blessing God gives us. We depend on sounds for much of what we learn, for talking to other people, and for enjoying the world around us. But not all sounds are sounds we want to hear. Sometimes we hear sounds we do not like or do not want to hear. **Noise** is unwanted, unpleasant, or unexpected sound.

noise (noiz)
unwanted, unpleasant, or unexpected sound

Noise can keep us awake at night. Noise can make it hard to study. Listening can be hard when a noise interferes with the sound we are trying to hear. Loud noises can scare us. When does sound become noise? What noises have you heard today?

Noise can be annoying and distracting, and noise can damage hearing. Very loud noises can cause pain. The pain is a warning that the noise is too loud. Noises which cause pain can break your eardrum. When your eardrum is broken, you cannot hear sounds as well.

Loud sounds which do not hurt can also cause hearing loss. But hearing loss does not always happen all at once. For example, people who work with loud machines can experience hearing loss after weeks or years of working near noisy machines. People who often listen to loud music may also experience hearing loss.

Sounds range from very soft to too loud. This chart shows some of the sounds at each level.

LEVEL	SOUNDS
very soft	sounds just barely heard: quiet whisper, rustling leaves
soft	humming, sound in a library
average	normal conversation, light traffic
loud	vacuum cleaner, heavy traffic
very loud	motorcycle, thunder clap, rock band
too loud	jet taking off, heavy machinery, explosions

Sounds at the loud and very loud levels can damage hearing if you listen to them for a long time. Noises at the very loud and too loud levels can cause pain. Sounds at the too loud level can damage hearing right away.

Sometimes sounds at the average and loud levels can cause problems. Loud noises or noises which are repeated over and over can cause headaches, make people crabby, and even make people tired. Often it is hard to think when there is noise nearby.

Too much noise is a problem in some places in the world today. In large cities, noise is part of our habitat. Cars, trucks, and buses create heavy traffic noise. Jet plane take-offs cause sonic booms which rattle windows. Machinery in factories and outdoors add to noise pollution.

People and governments try to control noise pollution in several ways. People who work near loud machines wear ear plugs or ear muffs to protect their ears. Many cities have laws which forbid trucks and noisy machines from operating during the evening and nighttime hours.

Sound insulation is material that sound cannot travel through easily. Cloth, rubber, fiberglass, and wood are sound insulators. In factories and schools, insulation helps control noise by stopping the sound waves from traveling out of a room, or into an area that should be kept quiet.

Does the Noise Help?

paper
pencil
a friend
clock with second hand

See how noise can make it difficult to concentrate.

1. Make up 10 simple math problems, or ask your teacher to suggest some from your math textbook.
2. Do the first 5 problems in a place where it is very quiet. Your partner should time you to see how long it takes. How long did it take?
3. Now have your partner make noise. Do the last 5 problems while your partner is being very noisy. How long does it take you now?

Why do you think people are supposed to be quiet in a library?

Controlling Noise Pollution

Noise can cause problems, even in your classroom. What can be done about noise?

1. Copy this chart. Listen for noises in your classroom. Fill in the chart to show the kinds and number of noises you hear.
2. Compare your list with those of other students.
3. What are some ways to control noise pollution? As a class project, decide how to control the noise in your room.

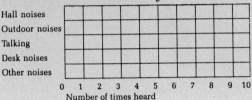

Hall noises	
Outdoor noises	
Talking	
Desk noises	
Other noises	

0 1 2 3 4 5 6 7 8 9 10
Number of times heard

Review

Summary

Sound is energy you can hear. Sound is produced when an object vibrates. The bigger the vibration, the louder the sound. The speed of the vibrations determines pitch. Noise can cause problems. There are ways for people to control noise pollution.

Vocabulary

sound   frequency
pitch   vibration
noise   resonance

Review Questions

1. How does resonance change loudness?
2. What three things determine the frequency of vibration—and therefore pitch?
3. What kinds of noise can damage hearing?
4. Give examples of ways to control noise pollution.

Chapter 3

Food Plants

What plant parts do people eat?
How is food prepared for eating?
What is a balanced diet?

Have you eaten a plant today?

Of course you have. Bread, oatmeal, cereal, mushrooms, pepper, lettuce, and apples are all parts of plants or are made from plants.

When God created the world, he said, " 'I give you every seed-bearing plant on the face of the whole earth and every tree that has fruit with seed in it. They will be yours for food' " (Gen. 1:29).

Food plants are important parts of our daily diets. Our bodies need food for its energy and to replace and add new and damaged parts of cells. Food keeps us alive and able to do God's work. The variety of flavors, colors, and textures of food helps us to enjoy God's creation.

Plant Parts

People usually do not eat all parts of a plant. There are five main plant parts that people might eat. They are roots, stems, leaves, fruits, and seeds (or nuts).

Roots

Sweet potatoes, turnips, carrots, radishes, and parsnips are different kinds of roots that people eat.

Root beer is made from the roots of the sassafras tree. Much of the sugar you eat comes from the root of the sugar beet.

What is your favorite root food?

Stems

People eat the stems of some plants. Asparagus, broccoli, and kohlrabi are plants having stems that people eat.

Strawberries are large, red stem ends. You might think that strawberries are fruits, but they're not. Look carefully at a strawberry. It has little seeds growing on it. A fruit has seeds *inside*, but a strawberry has seeds on little white veins outside.

Leaves

petiole (pet ´ē ōl) stalk that attaches a leaf to the stem

blade (blād) the broad, flattened part of a leaf

Plant leaves are made of two parts, the **petiole** and the **blade**. The petiole is the stalk that attaches a leaf to the stem. The blade is the broad, flattened part of the leaf. People eat only the petiole of some plants, only the blade of others.

People eat the petiole of the celery leaf. But they eat the blade of the cabbage. Rhubarb leaves are poisonous, but the rhubarb petiole is delicious.

Fruits

A fruit is the ripened part of a plant containing seeds. Apples, oranges, and bananas are fruits. So are tomatoes, pumpkins, cucumbers, and green peppers.

How many other fruits can you name?

Seeds and Nuts

Seeds are often found inside fruits. Sometimes people eat only the plant seeds. For example, rice, wheat, and beans are fruits, and people eat the seeds inside.

Nuts have thick shells and usually a single seed inside. People remove the shell of walnut, pecan, and chestnut fruits. They eat the seeds inside.

Growing Roots

4 radish seeds
potting soil
styrofoam cup

Find out more about roots by growing some tasty radishes. They take about four weeks to grow.

1. Punch two drain holes in the bottom of a styrofoam cup.
2. Fill the cup almost full of loose soil. Break up any lumps of dirt.
3. Put 3 or 4 radish seeds on top of the soil.
4. Cover with a thin layer of soil, and press the soil down lightly. Be sure the seeds are covered.
5. Water your seeds, but be careful not to soak them. Place the cup in a bright spot.
6. When your plants begin to grow, measure them each day. Keep track of their growth on a chart.
7. Keep the soil in your cup moist but not too wet. After four weeks, pull out the radishes. Clean them and eat them.

Focus on
George Washington Carver

George Washington Carver was born in the southern United States in 1864. His parents had been slaves before the Civil War.

Carver went to college, planning to become an artist, but he became a scientist instead. He became a college teacher himself, and he taught farmers that growing cotton every year took too many minerals from the soil. He told them to plant peanuts and sweet potatoes rather than cotton. When many farmers began growing these new crops, George Washington Carver studied ways to use peanuts and sweet potatoes. He invented over 100 ways to use sweet potatoes and over 300 ways to use peanuts.

For example, Carver used the sweet potato to make a kind of rubber and flour. From peanuts he made many products, including a substitute cheese, milk, and a type of wood stain.

George Washington Carver probably knew more about peanuts than anyone else in his time.

Fungus

fungus (fung´gəs) plants which do not make their own food

Fungus plants do not make their own food. They do not have any seeds, roots, stems, or leaves. Mush-

rooms and yeast are two examples of fungus plants that people eat.

Mushrooms get their energy from decaying organisms in the soil. Because mushrooms do not make food, they do not need light. In fact, they grow best in dark places. Some mushrooms are very good to eat, but others are extremely poisonous.

Yeast feeds on sugar. It is an important food. It makes bread rise, and without yeast all breads would be flat like crackers.

Herbs and Spices

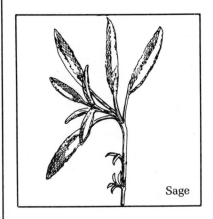
Sage

Oregano

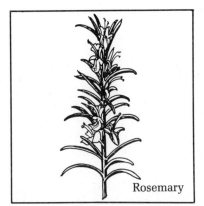
Rosemary

Pepper

Spices and herbs add flavor to many foods. Herbs and spices help make meals more interesting.

Herbs usually come from the leaves of plants.

Oregano, dill, sage, basil, and parsley are some common herbs. How many have you tasted?

Spices come from many different parts of plants. Spearmint, vanilla, mustard, ginger, nutmeg, rosemary, and cinnamon are some spices you might know. Pepper is also a spice, but salt is not. Even though salt is used to add flavor, it does not come from plants. Instead, salt comes from a mineral found in the ground or from evaporated salt water.

Focus on the Bible

Today many spices are easy to get. If you want some pepper or some cinnamon, you can buy them in any grocery store. But in Bible times, spices were very hard to get. Because different spices grow in many different parts of the world, the people in Bible times did not know many of the spices. Since spices were rare, they were valuable.

When rich kings and queens gave gifts, they gave gold and silver. They also gave spices. For example, the queen of Sheba gave Solomon "gold, large quantities of spices, and precious stones. There had never been such spices as those the queen of Sheba gave to King Solomon" (2 Chron. 9:9).

What a Variety!

1. Across the top of a piece of paper, write the names of each plant part that we eat.
2. List as many foods as you can think of in each category.
3. Circle your favorite one from each column.
4. Are there any that you do not like? Why do you think God created so many different kinds of food for people?

In Bible times spices were also used to keep food from spoiling, to cover the taste of spoiled food, and for medicine. Luke 23:55 to 24:3 describes another use for spices in Bible days.

Processing Food Plants

Some foods come to us right from the plant. The fresh fruits and vegetables you buy at the farmers' market or the grocery store are not processed but should be washed. In fact, you could grow some of these foods in your own yard.

Other plant foods are processed before you buy them. To **process** food means to prepare, treat, or change it in some way. Canned and frozen vegetables are cleaned and cut up before they are packed in water or frozen.

process (**pros** ´ es) to prepare, treat, or change food

Many foods are processed even more after they are brought home. For example, potatoes can be processed into mashed potatoes, French fries, or baked potatoes.

Grains are another kind of food that must be processed. Wheat is a grain that is ground into flour. Then the flour can be combined with other ingredients to make pancakes, bread, or brownies.

Peanuts are an example of how some foods are processed. The more a food is processed, generally the more it costs. Look at the chart to see how peanuts are processed.

Food Item	Process Steps
unshelled peanuts	washed
roasted shelled peanuts	shells removed, roasted
peanut butter	nuts crushed, oil added
peanut butter candy	chocolate added, shaped, wrapped

Our Bodies Use Food

Your body needs energy to live and to grow. Plants help provide you with energy. Your body takes energy from the plants and other food you eat and changes it to help you grow, move, and breathe.

nutrients(nōo´ trē ənts) ingredients that help build up the body

Plants provide nutrients. **Nutrients** are ingredients that help build up the body. Nutrients build healthy bones, muscles, and other organs. Water, vitamins, and minerals are some of the nutrients your body needs.

For good health, people need to eat foods from four basic food groups. These four food groups are dairy products, fruits and vegetables, grains, and meats.

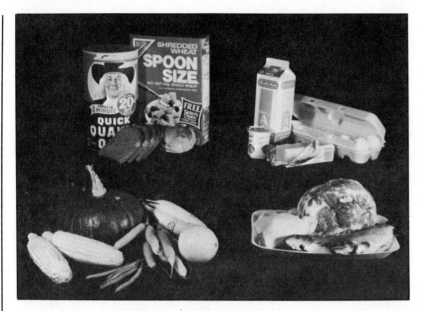

A balanced diet which includes these four food groups provides the energy and nutrients you need to be healthy. Which of the two food groups are plant foods?

Is Your Diet Balanced?

pencil
paper

If you eat foods from all four food groups every day, then you have a balanced diet. See if your diet includes food from each group.

1. Make 4 columns on your paper. Label each column with the name of a food group.
2. Try to remember everything you ate yesterday. Write the foods in the right columns.
3. You shouldn't worry if you don't have something in all four columns. People can get by for awhile without a certain food group. But it's a good idea to try to eat a balanced diet to grow and to stay healthy.

Food for the World

The lack of food and food nutrients is a problem in many counties of the world. Without proper foods people become sick and sometimes die.

About 10,000 people die of starvation every day. The very old and the very young die first. Of every five people in poor countries, three are poorly fed. They do not eat enough food or their diet is unbalanced, so they do not get enough protein, calories, vitamins, and minerals.

In rich countries like Canada and the United

Finding Nutrients

liquid starch
iodine solution
eye dropper
variety of plant foods
water
jar or cup

Starch is one of the nutrients found in food. You can test foods to see if they contain starch by using iodine solution.

1. Put a little liquid starch in a paper cup or baby food jar. Use the eyedropper to squeeze a few drops of iodine solution on the starch. When iodine solution mixes with starch it changes color.
2. Moisten a small piece of food with water.
3. Put a few drops of iodine solution on the wet food. If the iodine solution changes color, the food contains starch. Be sure to throw the food away so no one eats it. Iodine is a poison.
4. Test several foods. Find out which ones contain starch. Can you tell which ones have the most starch?

States there is plenty of food. But even in rich countries some people do not have enough money to buy the food they need.

Famines occur when there is not enough food in an area. Famines can be caused by the lack of rain, by floods, insect damage, storms, or war. During a famine thousands of people in a country may die of starvation. Many more become sick because of the lack of nutrients.

The map shows where famines have occurred in the past 30 years. In which parts of the world are famines common?

People in every country could grow and buy enough food if everyone worked together to help. In some places, better farming methods and tools could be used. In other places, wells and dams could provide water when there is not enough rain. Dams can help control floods as well as store water for energy and farming. The governments and people of the rich and poor countries can learn to work together to keep people from starving.

The Bible talks about how we should care for the poor. Read the following passages to find out what God wants us to do: Leviticus 19:9-10, Deuteronomy 15:1-6, Matthew 19:21, and Galatians 6:9-10.

Discuss the problem of hunger. Maybe your class or several classes can help one of the many organizations that are working to feed the hungry people of the world.

Review

Summary

People eat the roots, stems, leaves, fruits, and seeds of plants. People also eat mushrooms and yeast which are two kinds of fungus. These foods provide nutrients that people need to be healthy and to grow. Many of the people in poor countries lack enough food or the right kinds of food.

Vocabulary

petiole	process
blade	nutrients
fungus	

Review Questions

1. Give examples of each food plant group: root, stem, leaf, seed, fruit, fungus.
2. List a few herbs and spices.
3. What are the four food groups that people need for a balanced diet?

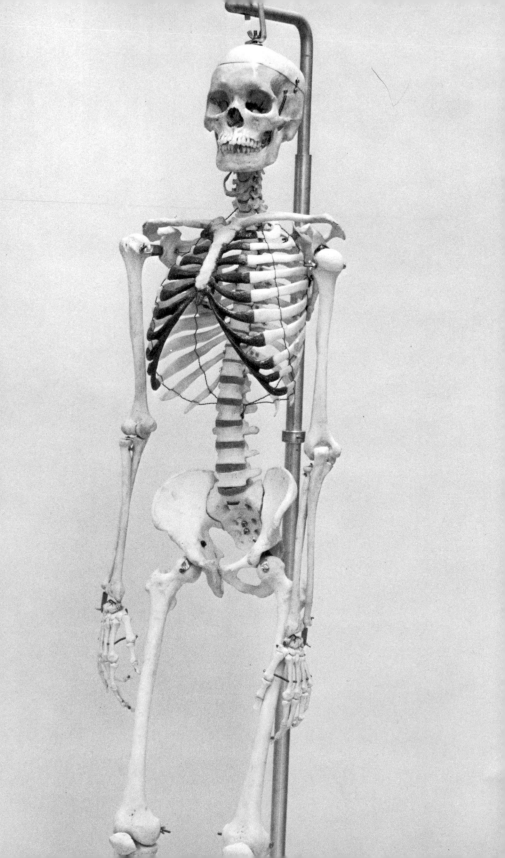

Chapter 4

Bones and Muscles

What are bones for?
How do muscles work?
What are tendons?

In Psalm 139:13-14, King David says that God made our bodies: "You knit me together in my mother's womb. I praise you because I am fearfully and wonderfully made; your works are wonderful, I know that full well."

All our bodies are similar in many ways. One of the ways that everyone is alike is that we all have bones and muscles. Bones hold our bodies up, and they protect parts of our bodies. Muscles make it possible for us to move. Muscles also move blood through our bodies, and they move food to and from our stomachs. Without bones and muscles we could not live.

Even though our bodies are similar in many ways, we are not all just the same. We all have bones and muscles, but your bones and muscles are different from somebody else's. Some people have large or long bones in their arms and legs. Other people are quite small. Some people's muscles are very strong. Other people are quite weak. Babies have more bones than grownups do. Men's muscles are often larger than women's. The bones in women's hips are shaped differently than in men's.

The differences in people's bodies give us different abilities. Large muscles make people strong. People with long bones are tall. The shape of women's hips makes it possible for them to carry and give birth to babies. The differences in our bodies show that we are all unique people.

Bones

skeleton (skel´ i t ən) a framework of bones

Your skeleton is the framework of your body. A **skeleton** is a framework of bones. Your skeleton holds everything in place. Hard skull bones hold and protect your brain. Your ribs protect the heart and lungs inside your chest. Most grownups have 206 bones in their skeletons. You have a few more than that. As you grow, the extra bones will grow together, and you will have 206 bones, too.

Your skeleton has several kinds of bones. Two of the kinds are flat bones and long bones. Your skull, shoulder blades, and hips are flat bones. Your arm and leg bones are long bones.

marrow (mar´ ō) soft material in bones, consisting of fat cells, blood cells, and tissue

Most of your long bones are hollow. Hollow bones provide strength without being too heavy. Inside the hollow bones is **marrow**. Bone marrow is the soft material consisting of fat cells, blood cells, and tissue, a center for blood cell production. The blood cells carry food to all parts of your body.

Blood also supplies food to your bones. Bones need energy to make new bone cells. Children's bones grow larger every year. Adults' bones do not grow larger, but they do change. Old bone cells are replaced with new bone cells all the time. In this way bones are kept strong.

Studying Bones

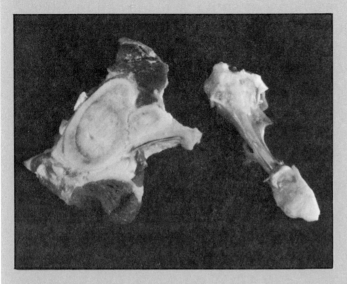

chicken or beef bone
magnifying lens

Look at bones to discover their parts. Try to use bones which still have some of the meat on them.

1. Study a chicken bone. Where did it attach to another bone? Crack the bone in half. Look for marrow inside.
2. Study a beef bone. Find the hard outside. This is bone. Is any softer marrow inside the bone?

Does the bone still have some meat on it? The meat is most likely muscle. Most of the meat we eat is muscle.

The Skull

Your skull is made of 28 flat bones. Small babies have spaces between some of their skull bones. These bones soon grow together. Your skull bones fit together so tightly they cannot move.

Sockets in the skull hold and protect your eyes. Other openings in the skull allow sound and air to pass through the skull into your body.

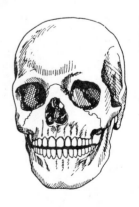

cartilage (kär´ tl ij) tough tissue that connects bones

The Spine

Your backbone, or spine, is made of a number of small bones. Between each of the bones is a pad of cartilage. **Cartilage** is tough tissue that connects bones. Cartilage cushions the bones of the spine and helps the spine bend.

Run your hands down the center of someone's back. Can you feel the bumpy bones?

The Rib Cage

Your ribs protect your heart and lungs. The ribs are twelve pairs of bones around your chest. The first ten pairs are attached to the spine in back and the breastbone in front. The last two pairs are attached just to the spine.

Run your fingers along your sides to feel your ribs.

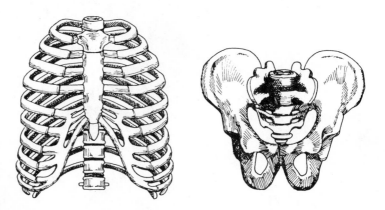

Hips

You have two hip bones. Together they form a shape like a bucket. Your hips make it possible for you to walk upright. They protect the body parts inside them. Your hips are connected to the bottom of your spine and the tops of your leg bones.

Legs and Feet

There are three main bones in each of your legs.
The basic form of the foot is similar to that of the hand. Can you move your feet and toes as easily as you can move your hands and fingers?

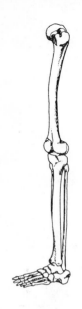

Arms and Hands

You have three long bones in each arm. The upper bone is connected to the shoulder blade. The two bones of your lower arm make it possible to twist your hands. You can hold your hands palms up or palms down because of the movement these bones make possible.

There are 27 bones in each of your hands. How many ways can you move your hands and wrists?

Other Bones

There are a number of other bones in your body. Each forms an important part of your skeleton.

Inside your ears are several small bones. They help you to hear.

Your teeth are attached to your jawbone. Put your hand on your chin. Open and close your mouth. Can you feel your jawbone move?

Can Your Rib Cage Move?

100 cm string
meter stick

1. Put a piece of string around a friend's chest.
2. Have your friend breathe in deeply. Measure how much string went around your friend's chest.
3. Ask the person to breathe out, and measure again.
4. Have your friend try the same exercise as you breathe in and out.

Muscles made the rib cage move, but the bones did not bend. Cartilage connects the bones of the rib cage. Cartilage is something like soft bone. It helps support parts of your body, but it is bendable.

You can see how this is possible by putting a rubber band around two pencils. You can move the pencils by stretching the rubber band. But the pencils themselves don't bend. The rubber band is like cartilage, and the pencils are like bones.

Draw Your Skeleton

kraft paper
crayons

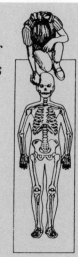

1. Lay on your back on a very large piece of paper. Have a partner trace around your body.
2. Cut out your paper body.
3. Use crayons to draw your skeleton on your paper body. Use the drawings in this book as a guide. Color in the bones.

How many different bones did you include? Can you name them?

Focus on Doctors

If you broke a bone, you would go to the doctor. Doctors help bones to heal.

First, the doctor takes an X-ray which shows how the bone is broken. If the broken bone is a rib or toe, the doctor will probably do nothing. These bones heal best when left alone.

When an arm, leg, or finger bone is broken, the doctor will probably put on a cast or splint. These bones heal best when the muscles cannot move them. Casts and splints hold the bones still.

If the bone is badly broken, the doctor may have to put the pieces of the bone back together. Sometimes doctors do surgery on broken bones, putting them together with screws or metal rods.

God made it possible for bones to heal themselves. Whatever method the doctor uses to help hold the broken bone in place, it's God who created bones so that they would form new bone tissue over and around the broken part.

Joints

Your skeleton is a system of bones. The bones are connected to each other with joints. A **joint** is a place at which two bones are joined. Your skeleton has several kinds of joints.

The bones of your skull are joined by joints which do not move. They are connected something like a jigsaw puzzle.

Your arms and legs are connected to your body by ball and socket joints. Ball and socket joints allow you to move in circles, back and forth, and up and down. Try moving your arm all these ways.

joint a point where two bones are joined

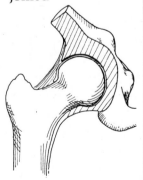

Many of your joints are hinge joints. The joints in your fingers, elbows, and knees are hinge joints. They allow up and down movement.

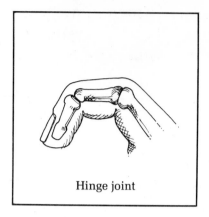

Hinge joint

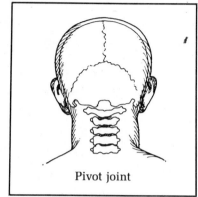

Pivot joint

The joint that moves your head can move in two directions. Your skull is attached to your spine with a pivot joint. It allows movement up and down and in a circle. But it does not move as much as a ball and socket joint.

All these joints are held together by ligaments. **Ligaments** are like rubber bands, stretchy, but tough. Ligaments hold bones together, but they allow the bones to move.

Bones, ligaments, and joints work together to support and protect your body, and to make movement possible. They are your body's framework.

ligament (lig´ ə mənt) tough, stretchy tissue which connects bones

Focus on Animal Skeletons

God created fish and animal skeletons. He didn't make them all alike. Each kind of animal has a special skeleton designed for its needs.

Birds have very light skeletons. Their bones are hollow. Light, hollow bones make it possible for birds to fly.

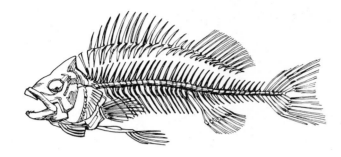

Fish do not need strong bones for support. The water helps support their bodies. So fish have very small flexible bones.

Large, strong leg bones help kangaroos jump. Elephants need huge bones to support their great weight.

A frog has very long bones in its feet so that it can jump more easily.

Muscles

When you close your eyes, bend a finger or take a step, your muscles are working. There are more than 600 muscles in your body. Muscles are attached to your bones. Muscles move the bones of your skeleton.

Muscles also pump blood and move food through your body.

Muscles are tissues of fibers. The fibers are long and thin like threads. Muscle tissue can be contracted and relaxed. A relaxed muscle is long and thin. When it is contracted, it becomes shorter and thicker.

The muscles attached to your skeleton are the ones which make movement possible. When a mus-

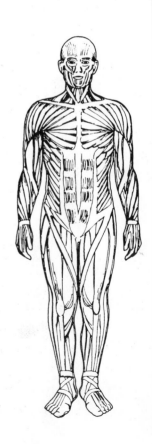

cle is contracted or becomes shorter, it pulls a bone. The bone moves at the joint.

Muscles work in pairs to move your skeleton. When one of the pair contracts, the other relaxes.

Make a Bone and Muscle Model

paper fastener
tape
heavy cardboard
paper

You can better understand how muscles work by making a model of bones and muscles.

1. Cut two rectangles from cardboard. Each rectangle should be 30 x 4 cm.
2. Connect the ends of the cardboard pieces with a paper fastener.
3. Take two sheets of paper. Fold them in half. Fold again. Fold again.
4. Cut and fold the two pieces of paper as shown.

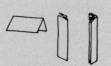

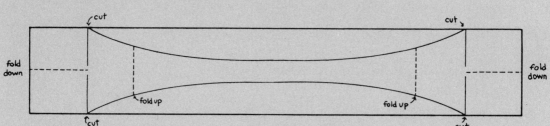

5. Tape the two paper muscles to the cardboard bones as shown.
6. Hold one bone still. Move the other bone up and down. Watch how the muscles move. In the same way, the muscles in your body contract and relax as they move your bones.

The muscles in your arm show how muscles work in pairs. One muscle contracts to raise your arm. The other muscle contracts to lower it again.

Muscles are attached to the bones by tendons. **Tendons** are tough cords or bands that connect muscle to bone. Tendons do not stretch.

Place your hand palm down on the desk. Move your fingers as if you are playing the piano. Watch the tendons move in the back of your hand. These tendons are connected to the muscles and bones of your hand and fingers. They move when you move your hand.

Muscles do several important jobs. You already know that they move your bones so you can move. Muscles help you hold and lift things. The muscles in your face and throat help you chew and eat.

Muscles do one other important thing. They help keep you warm. Muscles act like a layer of insulation beneath the skin. They help keep the heat inside your body. They can also make heat. When you shiver, it is because the muscles are moving quickly. They are burning energy to make heat. Your muscles are trying to warm you up when you shiver.

Not all of the muscles in your body have the job of moving bones. One muscle—your heart—has the job of moving blood to all parts of your body. Another important muscle that does not move bones is the tongue. Why is this muscle important?

You control most of the muscles in your body. When you want to move your arm, your brain sends a message to the muscles. Then your muscles contract to move your arm. But you do not control some muscles. For example, you do not control your heart muscle. It contracts and relaxes in a regular rhythm. You cannot stop it or control its beating.

tendon (ten´ dən) cord which connects muscles to bones

This Sure Is Complicated!

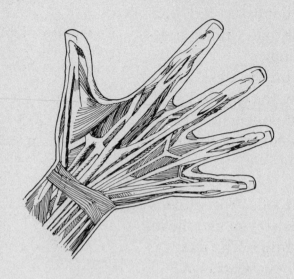

paper clip
pencil
paper

1. Look at this picture of the wrist and hand.
2. Lay your arm flat on your desk with your fingers spread out. Put the paper clip close to your hand.
3. Close your fingers together. How did you do that? Did you use bones, muscles, cartilage, ligaments, or tendons? Did you have to think about moving each of those?
4. Try to pick up the paper clip by only moving one part (bone, or muscle, or tendon, or ligament, or cartilage) at a time. Can you do it?
5. Write down every part that you use to pick up a paper clip.

If you think this is complicated, just think of all the different parts of your body that must work together when you climb a ladder, kick a ball, or pick up a wastebasket.

Even the most simple things can involve many different parts of the body.

Caring for Your Bones and Muscles

Our bodies are part of God's wonderful creation. And God wants us to use our bodies in ways which please him.

Good nutrition helps your bones and muscles work well and grow. Exercise is important, too. If you do not get enough exercise, your muscles become weak. People with weak muscles can more easily injure muscles, ligaments, and bones. That is because muscles need exercise to stay loose and flexible.

Much of your exercise comes from playing. When you run, swim, play ball, or ride your bicycle, you are exercising. Be sure you get enough exercise every day to build strong, healthy muscles.

Heart Exercise

1. Find your heartbeat (pulse) either in your neck or on your wrist.
2. Count how many times your heart beats in one minute. Write it down.
3. Do jumping jacks for 2 minutes.
4. Count how many times your heart beats in one minute again. Did it go up very much?

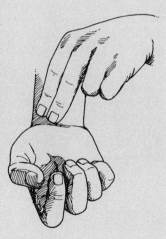

The higher your pulse, the harder your heart had to work.

But your heart stays strong if you exercise often. In fact, the more your heart works, the stronger it gets.

Review

Summary

Your skeleton is a system of bones which support and protect your body. Bones are attached to each other at joints which allow movement. Ligaments hold bones together. Muscles move the bones of the skeleton.

Vocabulary

marrow	skeleton
tendon	joint
ligament	cartilage

Review Questions

1. Name two kinds of bones.
2. What jobs do bones do?
3. Name the different kinds of joints.
4. How do muscles move bones?
5. What other jobs do muscles do?

Chapter 5

Weather

How are clouds formed?
What is air pressure?
What makes the wind blow?

What is the weather like today? Is it sunny or cloudy? Warm or cold? Windy or calm? Is it raining or snowing? What it is like outdoors is called the weather.

The weather shows God's power. God created the weather, and he controls it. You can read about God's control of the weather in the following Bible passages: 1 Samuel 12:17-18, Job 28:23-27, Matthew 8:23-28, and Genesis 9:12-16. What do these passages tell us about God?

Weather affects all living things. It determines if you wear a bathing suit or a winter coat. It can help plants grow, or it can kill them. How animals live is affected by the weather, too. What are some things animals do because of the weather?

Without rain and sun, plants could not grow. Without snow, lakes and rivers would dry up. The weather also provides us with much beauty. Sunny days, high-flying clouds, and rain are all gifts from God.

Weather occurs in the atmosphere. The **atmosphere** is the layer of air around the earth.

Weather is caused by the sun's energy. When sunlight strikes the earth, it warms the ground. As the ground becomes warm, it warms the air above it. All of our weather—wind, rain, storms and snow—are a

atmosphere (at´ mə sfîr) the layer of air around the earth

75

result of the sun's energy.

The way the sun's light strikes the earth helps determine temperature. In summer, sunlight strikes the earth straight on. In winter it reaches the earth at an angle. That is why the temperatures are higher in summer than in winter.

Summer

Winter

How Hot Is It?

tape
styrofoam cup
thermometer

How does the surface of the earth affect the temperature of the air? Try this activity to find out.

1. Poke a thermometer through the bottom of a styrofoam cup. Leave about 3 cm of the thermometer inside the cup. Tape the thermometer to the cup so it will not slide.
2. Measure the temperature in several places.
   • over grass in the sun
   • over concrete in the sun
   • over blacktop in the sun
   • over grass in the shade
   • over concrete in the shade
   • over blacktop in the shade
3. Was the temperature higher in the sunlight or in the shade? How do light and dark surfaces make a difference in the temperature?

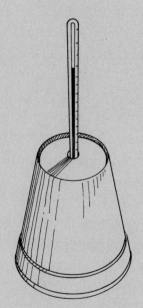

76

Rain and Snow

Water falls on the earth in different forms. Rain, snow, sleet, and hail are all forms of **precipitation**. Precipitation is the process of water droplets falling from the clouds to earth.

There is always water in the air. Water from oceans and lakes is always evaporating into the air. In **evaporation**, water changes into vapor or tiny water particles in the air.

As the moist air from lakes and oceans moves over the land, it is warmed by the earth and rises high into the atmosphere. It reaches and produces the clouds. This is how water from the earth gets into the clouds.

High in the atmosphere, the air is cold. The lower temperature causes the water particles to separate from the air and form droplets. The process of water particles in the air joining together to form droplets is called **condensation**.

At first the water droplets in the clouds are small. As they grow larger, the water drops become too heavy. They fall to earth as precipitation. In warm weather, rain falls. In the winter, it snows. If the water freezes as it condenses, it may fall as sleet or hail.

precipitation (pri sip´ i tā´ shən) the process of water droplets falling from the clouds to earth

evaporation (i vap´ ə rā´ shən) the change of water into vapor in the air

condensation (kon´ den sā´ shən) the process of tiny particles in the air joining to form water droplets

On the earth, the water collects in streams and rivers. It flows down to the sea. Once again the water is part of the ocean where it began its journey.

The water cycle is God's plan for providing water for the living things on the earth.

Humidity

humidity (hyoo mid´ i tē) the amount of water in the air

The amount of water in the air is called **humidity**. We say that the humidity is high when there is a lot of water in the air. The humidity is low when the air is not very damp.

The morning dew is related to humidity. When the humidity is high, the water in the night air condenses on cooler objects. This water is the dew you find on the grass in the morning. Frost occurs if dew freezes.

Everyday Humidity

glass drinking cup
ice cubes
water

1. Fill a glass drinking cup with ice cubes.
2. Pour cold water in the cup until it is almost full. Be sure that no water spills on the outside of the cup.
3. Watch for a couple of minutes. Is water collecting on the outside of the cup? If the cup only gets damp on the outside, the humidity is low. If water drops form and run down the side of the cup, then the humidity is very high.

Understanding Humidity

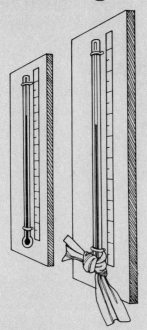

2 thermometers
1 piece of shoestring or cloth
water
notebook

Here's a more precise way to measure humidity.

1. Attach a piece of shoestring to the bulb of the first thermometer. Wet the shoestring with water.
2. Place both thermometers together on a wall.
3. Fan the thermometers with the notebook. (Do not blow on them.) Record the temperature readings on the two thermometers.

The difference in readings between the two thermometers indicates humidity. If the readings are the same, there is as much water in the air as in the shoestring. That shows that the humidity is very high. If there is a 15° difference between the two readings, the humidity is very low. Your reading is probably between these two extremes. The larger the difference, the lower the humidity.

Do your thermometers show high or low humidity?

Clouds

Clouds are an important part of the weather. They can bring snow or rain. They can block the sun's light. And they can work like a blanket to hold the atmosphere's heat near the earth.

Before clouds can form, three things must be present: water in the air, rising air, and particles like dust, ice, or smoke. As the moist air rises high into the atmosphere, it becomes cooler. When the moisture in the air condenses, the water droplets and the other particles form clouds.

The kind of clouds which are formed depends on how high they are and what they contain.

stratus (strā´ təs) clouds that hang in low, flat sheets

Low, flat sheets of clouds are called **stratus** clouds. They are grey, heavy clouds, and often bring rain.

cumulus (kyōo´ myə ləs) billowy white clouds

Located higher than stratus clouds are **cumulus** clouds. Cumulus clouds are billowy and white. They look like popcorn in the sky. Cumulus are fair weather clouds. Heaps of cumulus clouds sometimes reach high into the sky. On a sunny summer day, it is fun to lie on your back and look for animal shapes in cumulus clouds.

The highest clouds are **cirrus**. They look like white, feathery wisps. Cirrus clouds are formed with ice particles. Cirrus clouds are fair weather clouds, too.

Stratus, cumulus, and cirrus are the three main kinds of clouds. The many other clouds are really types of these three.

cirrus (sir´ əs) high, feathery clouds

The Blanket

pencil
paper

What is the relationship between temperature and clouds? Keep track of the clouds for a week or two to find out.

1. Just before you go to bed, go outside. Measure the temperature with a thermometer.
2. Check to see if the sky is clear, partly cloudy, or completely cloudy.
3. Do this for a week or two. Make sure it is about the same time each night. Write down the temperature and the amount of clouds on a chart. Is it usually warmer when it is clear or cloudy? Do the clouds act like blankets?

Date	Time	Temperature	Clouds

Focus on Meteorologists

Scientists who study the weather are called meteorologists. They study temperature, wind, precipitation, humidity, clouds, and air pressure. They study all parts of the weather. Meteorologists use weather maps and pictures taken by satellites. They use computers to help them understand the information they gather.

Then meteorologists try to tell what kind of weather is coming. Many people depend on meterorologists. Farmers need to know what the

Charting the Weather

thermometer
paper
pencil

Keep track of the weather as a class to find out how weather changes.

1. Copy this chart.

DAY	TEMPERATURE high temp. in degrees Celsius	PRECIPITATION rain, snow, dew, frost, hail, sleet	WIND light breeze, calm, heavy wind, etc.	CLOUDS name of clouds, and whether partly cloudy, clear, etc.
M				
T				
W				
T				
F				

2. Put a thermometer outdoors, near your classroom.
3. Check the weather every day and keep track on the chart. Read the thermometer at the same time each day. Look at the clouds. Check the wind. What weather patterns can you observe?

weather will be. If a storm is coming, the farmers try to harvest their crops before rain and winds ruin the plants. Airports hire meteorologists to tell them when the weather is too dangerous for airplanes to fly. Even your school principal depends on meteorologists to tell when to close school because of the weather.

Meteorologists are able to predict the weather because the weather obeys God's laws. God created the weather and made laws for the weather to follow. You know it will not snow on the warmest day of summer because God's laws are orderly and predictable. Wind and rain, heat and cold, snow and clouds all follow the laws God provided for them. When people understand how God created and controls the weather, they can begin to tell what the weather will be like.

Meteorologists work in many different jobs. Some work for radio and television stations and give weather reports on the news. Some meteorologists work for the government. They issue weather reports to warn of storms or hurricanes.

Despite all the progress in studying the weather, there are still some surprises. That's because weather depends on many different factors.

Air Movement

The air around us is always moving. Moving air in the atmosphere is called wind. Winds may be as gentle as a breeze or as strong as a hurricane.

Wind is caused by differences in air pressure and temperature.

Air is made up of particles. The particles of air push down on the earth's surface.

When air is heated, the air particles move farther

low pressure condition in which particles are farther apart in warm air

high pressure condition in which particles are closer together in cool air

apart. Warm air is not as heavy. This is called **low pressure**. When the air is cold, the particles are closer together. The heavier cold air is said to have **high pressure**.

An **air mass** is a large body of air having the same temperature and humidity. The movement of air masses causes changes in the weather.

Cold air masses have higher air pressure than

Observing Air Pressure

glass jar
eye dropper
plastic wrap
rubber bands

How does air pressure work? Try this activity to find out.

1. Fill a jar to within 3 cm of the top with water.
2. Fill an eye dropper with water. Slowly squeeze water from the eyedropper until it will float just above the water surface.
3. Leave the eye dropper floating in the water. Stretch the plastic wrap tightly over the mouth of the jar. Hold it in place with rubber bands.
4. Gently press the plastic wrap down with your finger tips. Be careful not to break the wrap. Observe what happens.

When you press on the plastic wrap, you push the air inside the jar into a smaller area. This increases the air pressure in the jar.

warm air masses. When two air masses meet, the cooler air mass pushes the warmer one. The warm air rises and is pushed away. The cold air mass moves into the area where the warm air was.

When an air mass moves slowly, we feel a breeze. If the air mass moves quickly, we feel a strong wind. Air movement is a result of differences in air pressure between warm and cold air masses.

air mass a large body of air

How Is an Air Mass Made?

2 thermometers
2 styrofoam cups
2 bowls
hot water
ice cubes
tape

What difference do you think there would be in air masses that form over the ocean by the equator and over the Arctic Ocean? The following activity may help you guess.

1. Fill one bowl with ice, and fill the other with hot water.
2. Put the bowls in a place where there will not be air movement.
3. Poke a thermometer through the bottom of each cup. Tape it in place so it will not slide.
4. Hold the thermometer over each bowl for 5 minutes.
5. What was the temperature over each bowl after 5 minutes?

Make a Weather Vane

straight pin
plastic straw
posterboard or tag board
cardboard (14 x 22 cm)
pencil (with eraser)
clay

Some people tell which way the wind is blowing by licking a finger and holding it up in the breeze. Here is a more precise way to find the direction of the wind.

1. Mark north, south, east, and west on the sides of the cardboard.

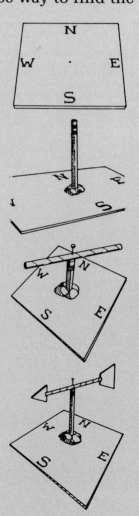

2. Poke the point of the pencil into the center of the cardboard. Press clay around it to hold it in place.

3. Push a straight pin through the straw and into the eraser on the pencil.

4. Cut slits into both ends of the straw.

5. Cut a head and tail for the vane from the posterboard. Put them into the slits in the straw.

Take your weather vane outdoors. Place it where the wind will reach it. Be sure that "north" on the card is facing north. When the wind is blowing, your weather vane should point at the direction from which the wind is coming.

Fronts

A **front** is the leading edge of an air mass. It is the line where two masses meet. A cold front is the beginning of a cold air mass. A warm front is the beginning of a warm air front.

When a front passes through the area where you live, it brings a change in the weather. The temperature will change. Precipitation and storms are often found along fronts. And the wind may change direction and speed.

Cold fronts move quickly. Their high pressure pushes into an area. Cold fronts usually pass in a

front the leading edge of an air mass

few hours. Warm fronts move more slowly. They are moving because they have been pushed out of another area or pulled along by a cold front. A slow moving warm front may take days to pass by.

Focus on The Chinook Wind

In many places in the world, special winds are caused by the shape of the land. For example, the Rocky Mountains in the United States and Canada cause a special wind. Years ago the Indians called this wind "snow eater." Today it is called the chinook (shi **nook´**) wind.

As moist air from the ocean reaches the mountains it is forced upwards. The air near the top of the mountains is cooler. As the moist ocean air nears the mountain tops, water condenses and it rains or snows.

After losing its moisture, the air becomes very dry. As the dry wind blows down the mountain slopes, it is warmed by the rocky mountainside. When the chinook wind reaches the plains the temperature goes up, and the dry air soaks up moisture from the ground. A cold winter's day can become a nice warm day. If the chinook wind passes over snowfields, it can "eat" or evaporate as much as 60 cm of snow in one day.

Storms

There is a great deal of energy in the air. Wind,

rain, air pressure, and air masses all contain energy. It is easy to see this energy in storms.

When warm, wet air rises quickly, the water droplets in the clouds can become charged with electricity. The electricity jumps between clouds or from the clouds to the ground.

Tornadoes can be caused by the collision of warm and cold air masses. When rapidly rising warm air begins to spin, a funnel cloud can form. Tornadoes occur when the humidity is high and the temperature is above 25° C in the warm air mass that collides with a cold air mass.

Tropical storms form over the oceans. In tropical storms, high winds move in a circular path. At the center of the winds is the eye of the storm. Here it is completely calm. When the winds of a tropical storm blow at more than 120 km per hour, it is called a hurricane.

Another kind of storm is a blizzard. Winter blizzards combine high winds and blowing snow with low temperatures. Blizzards may have winds blowing at 70 km an hour.

The right amounts of rain and snow are important to the earth. Rain helps plants grow. Snow melts in the spring and waters the earth as it runs off into rivers and streams. But too much rain causes flooding. It can wash away the soil that plants need. It can damage roads and homes. When there is too much snow or when it melts too quickly, swollen rivers can cause much damage.

Hail can be very dangerous. These hard balls of ice can be as small as peas, or as large as tennis balls. Hail can ruin fruit on trees, flatten crops in the fields, and even kill people and animals. Exodus 9:18-26 tells what happened when God sent hail to Egypt.

Changing Weather

People can change the weather, but the changes aren't always positive. The smog in large cities is an example of a harmful change in the weather. Los Angeles, California, is a large city that has smog. The word smog comes from the words **sm**oke and **fog** because it is a smoky kind of fog.

Los Angeles is located between the ocean and the mountains. Winds from the ocean trap the smog against the mountains. The smog can't get over the mountains or blow out to sea, so it hangs over the city. Sometimes a heavy blanket of smog hangs over Los Angeles for days at a time.

In California, laws now control how much pollution cars and factories can put into the air. The lawmakers hope this will help to control the smog.

Los Angeles is not the only place where people have affected the weather. In fact, some scientists believe that weather is changing all over the world because of people. Think about all the cars, factories, and houses in the world. Each one puts some pollution into the air by burning gas, coal, or oil. All of this pollution goes into the air.

Scientists think that pollution may be changing the amount of sunlight that shines on the earth. It may also hold too much of the earth's heat in like a blanket. God created the balance beween the amount of heat we get from the sun and the amount of heat we lose into space. Scientists are not certain what will happen when the balance God made is changed, but they are worried that the earth's weather might change.

Scientists are certain about one of the changes pollution is causing. In North America and in Europe factories put pollution into the air. Winds blow the pollution over many kilometers. The pollution is picked up by rain which falls on forests and lakes. The pollution enters the water cycle. This pollution is called acid rain.

Acid rain which falls on the forests is causing trees to become sick and die. Acid rain in lakes and rivers is killing fish. Some lakes have received so much acid rain that all the fish in these lakes have died.

Acid rain shows the effects people can have on weather and on the water cycle when they change the balance in God's creation.

After the flood, God made a promise to Noah. That promise is also for you and me. God said, " 'As long as the earth endures, seedtime and harvest, cold and heat, summer and winter, day and night will never cease' " (Gen. 8:22).

We know we will always have the seasons and the changes in the weather which spring, summer, winter, and fall bring. That is a promise from God.

But we still need to be concerned about the weather. When we change the weather, it can be very harmful. What should Christians do to care for God's gift of weather?

Acid Rain

elodea (or other aquarium plant)
2 jars (about 1 liter size)
water
vinegar

Find out about the effects of acid rain on the environment.

1. Fill the jars almost full with water.
2. Place plants in each jar.
3. Label one jar "ACID."
4. Put both jars in the sunlight.
5. Add about 10 ml of vinegar to the jar labeled acid. Do this once each day. Vinegar is an acid that is like acid rain.
6. Observe the changes in the "acid" jar. How do the plants look after a week? Why do you think this is happening?

Review

Summary

The weather is what the conditions outdoors are like. Precipitation falls from the clouds in the form of rain or snow. Humidity, the amount of water in the air, can cause dew or frost. The air around us is constantly moving. Its movement is caused by air pressure. Clouds are formed by water, rising air, and particles like dust, ice, or smoke. The weather affects all living things.

Vocabulary

precipitation	atmosphere
condensation	humidity
evaporation	stratus
low pressure	cirrus
cumulus	high pressure
air mass	front

Review Questions

1. How does the angle of sunlight striking the earth affect temperature?
2. Why are rain and snow important?
3. What is air pressure?
4. How does the weather affect our lives?

Chapter 6

The Oceans

How large are the oceans?
What is the ocean floor like?
What is plankton?

The world's oceans are the great bodies of salt water which cover most of the earth.

Have you ever been to the **ocean**? Maybe you live near an ocean. What is the ocean like? What plants and animals live in the ocean?

ocean (ō´ shən) the mass of salt water that covers the earth

In the Bible, oceans are called "seas." When God created the world, he created the seas, too. Read about the creation of the seas in Genesis 1:6, 7, 9, 10, 20, 21, and 22.

Psalms 93 and 95 talk about the sea. To whom does the sea belong? Do you think the Psalmist ever saw the sea? Why? What does the Psalmist say about the sea?

What can the ocean teach us about God?

Ocean Water

The ocean is part of the earth's water cycle. As rain falls onto land, it collects in streams. Streams carry the water to rivers, and the rivers finally empty into the ocean.

Along the way, water picks up material from the land and from the river bottoms. The water carries this material with it into the ocean. All kinds of minerals found on earth, many dissolved gasses, sand, and other materials are carried to the ocean.

Over time, more and more minerals are added to the ocean water. The most important material in ocean water is salt. Because of the salt in ocean water, people cannot drink ocean water. Things float more easily in ocean water than in other water. Ocean water does not freeze at 0° C because of its salt.

When the water evaporates into the air to begin the water cycle again, the salt and other minerals are left behind in the ocean.

Locating the Oceans

globe

Some people think there is one great ocean. Others say there are five oceans. There is not a right or wrong answer to how many oceans there are. It depends on how you look at the world.

1. Look at a globe. Find the areas of land and of water.
2. Is there more land or water?
3. Find the names of the oceans. Are the oceans connected?
4. What other bodies of water can you find? What are some of their names?
5. Which oceans are located near the country in which you live?

The Ocean's Role in the Water Cycle

small dish
clear cup (glass or plastic)
hot water
ice cubes

Try to construct a model of how the water cycle works.

1. Fill a cup half full of hot water.
2. Fill a dish with ice cubes. Set the dish on the top of the glass.
3. After 5 minutes, what do you see happening on the bottom of the dish?

Imagine that the water in the glass is the ocean, and the ice cubes in the dish are the cold air of the atmosphere. When ocean water evaporates, it is cooled in the air as it rises. As it cools, it forms water droplets. What would happen to the water cycle if this did not happen?

Freezing the Ocean

water
2 plastic containers
thermometer
salt
freezer

Many large lakes and most small ones freeze over in the winter. Why doesn't the ocean freeze like that? Is it because of the salt in the water? Try to find out.

1. Fill two plastic containers with equal amounts of water.

2. Label one container "ocean," and add a tablespoon of salt to the water in that container. Stir the water until the salt is dissolved. Keep adding small amounts of salt until it will not dissolve anymore.
3. Put both containers in the freezer.
4. Check the temperature of each one every 20 minutes. What temperature does the fresh water freeze at? What temperature does the ocean water freeze at?

Understanding Ocean Water

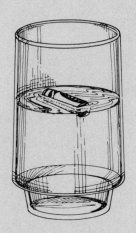

200 ml water
20 ml salt
½ crayon
cup or glass

Salt water is not good to drink, and it doesn't freeze quickly. In what other ways is ocean water different from clear water?

1. Fill a glass half full with water.
2. Put half a crayon into the water. Watch what happens to the crayon.
3. Take the crayon out of the water. Add 20 ml of salt to the water. Stir it until the salt is dissolved.
4. Put the crayon back into the water. What happens to the crayon now?

The Ocean Floor

What is the ocean bottom like? The ocean floor is much like the land. It has mountains and valleys, hills and plains. When underwater mountains reach above the surface of the ocean, they form islands.

The ocean near the land is shallow. The slanting ocean floor beyond the shore is called the **continental shelf**. The water above the shelf is teeming with life. Most of the ocean's fish live on the continental shelf. Many ocean plants grow here, too.

Beyond the shelf, the ocean floor drops off suddenly. The ocean becomes very deep. Not as many fish live in the deep ocean water because it is colder and darker.

At its deepest point, the Marianas Trench, the ocean is more than 11 kilometers deep. No light reaches the ocean floor here. If there were no salt in the water, it would turn to ice at this depth.

continental shelf (kon´ tə **nen**´ tl shelf) the slanting area beyond the shore

Ocean Life

You already know that there are different kinds of plant and animal communities on the land. There are also different communities in the ocean.

Seaweeds are important food producers for ocean communities. Seaweeds grow along the shore and on the continental shelf. Plants can only grow where light can reach them through the water. **Kelp**

kelp large brown seaweed

is a kind of seaweed that is large and brown. Most kinds of kelp grow to over 20 meters tall. The communities which live on and above the continental shelf depend on seaweeds like kelp to be the food producers for those communities.

Out in the open ocean and in the deep waters of the ocean, plankton are the basic food. **Plankton** are tiny plants and animals that are free-floating organisms in the water. Animal plankton eat plant plankton. There are billions of plankton in the ocean because they are the food for ocean communities.

There are more than 20,000 kinds of fish and animals that live in the sea. Most live on the continental shelf where the water is warmed by the sun and seaweed is plentiful.

Focus on Jacques Cousteau

Jacques Cousteau is an oceanographer. He has spent his life studying the ocean. Cousteau invented the aqualung, a machine which lets divers breathe underwater. Cousteau has written several books about the sea, and he has made many television programs and films about the plants and animals which live in the ocean.

Jacques Cousteau travels the oceans in his ship, the *Calypso*. For many years, Cousteau has tried to teach people about the need to take care of the ocean and the creatures that live there.

Ocean Resources

The ocean holds many resources for people. The most important resource is the ocean's water itself. By means of the water cycle, God uses the ocean to provide an ever-fresh supply of water to the earth.

Many foods come from the ocean. Cod, haddock, herring, and other fish are caught on the continental shelf. Clams, lobsters, and oysters are also caught in these shallow waters. Tuna and other fish are caught in the deep waters far from shore.

Fish provide other products besides food. Some fish are ground up for use as plant food or as food for cattle.

Kelp can be used in many ways. It is put into some candies and medicines. Kelp can also be used for food and is a good source of minerals.

Ocean water contains many minerals. Salt can be removed from water by evaporation. Iodine and other minerals can also be taken from the water in this way. But most minerals cannot be easily removed from ocean water.

Many parts of the continental shelf contain rich deposits of oil and gas. Huge oil drilling rigs are used to get these energy sources from the ocean floor.

The ocean and its plants and animals are important resources for people. Many scientists believe that in the years ahead even more of our food and energy will come from the sea. It is important for people to take care of the ocean resources.

Focus on Whale Hunting

Many years ago, only the Inuit tribe hunted whales. They used hand-held harpoons and hunted in small boats, called kayaks. Later, people used large boats and harpoon guns. They were able to kill many more whales than the Inuit had.

Today, people hunt whales in huge ships called whaling vessels. They use harpoons which explode after they hit the whale. This new technology has allowed people to kill even more whales.

Many people believe that too many whales have been killed. They are afraid that whales may become extinct.

The ocean needs whales. Some whales feed on plankton, and others eat squid. If there were no whales to control the numbers of these organisms, we are not certain what would happen to the balance in the ocean community.

Technology made it easier for people to hunt whales. Misuse of this technology made it possible to kill too many whales.

Understanding Water Pollution

water
10 ml motor oil
paper cup
feather or piece of cloth

When an oil tanker sinks or spills its oil, a large area of the ocean can be polluted. Oil can spread over the water and pollute the water, kill birds and fish, and damage the shoreline. See what effect oil spills can have.

1. Fill a cup half full with water. Pour 10 ml of oil on top of the water. Do not stir or shake the cup.
2. What happens to the oil? Does it mix into the water?
3. Dip a feather or a piece of cloth into the water. Try not to get any oil on it. What happens to the feather? Can you clean and dry the feather?
4. Now try to remove the oil from the cup without removing any of the water. How will you do it?

When oil spreads over a large area of the ocean, it is very hard to remove. It sticks to birds' feathers so they cannot fly, and it pollutes the water fish use.

Caring for the Oceans

People are responsible for how they use the ocean. The ocean is part of God's creation, and God wants people to use the ocean resources for food and energy. He also wants people to care for the water and the organisms of the ocean.

When tankers spill oil on the ocean, it is hard to clean up. When people dump garbage and chemicals into the water, they pollute the oceans. When people hunt or kill too many animals, the balance God created can be upset. When the balance in a community is changed, all organisms may be affected.

Scientists are still discovering many things about the ocean. Because the ocean is so huge and so deep, it is more difficult for scientists to study the ocean than the land. But as we learn more about the ocean, we also learn more about how to care for it.

Review

Summary

Most of the earth is covered by oceans. Ocean water is salty and contains many other minerals. The ocean floor is somewhat like the land: it has mountains, valleys, and plains. Many plants and animals live in the oceans. People get food and other products from the oceans. It is important to learn to care for the oceans.

Vocabulary

continental shelf   kelp

plankton   ocean

Review Questions

1. How do minerals get into the ocean?
2. How do people use kelp?
3. What resources does the ocean provide to people?
4. Why is it important to study the ocean?

Chapter 7

Machines and Work

What is a machine?
How does an inclined plane work?
What is technology?

What kinds of work do you do?

All people do work. Work is part of God's plan for people. God created people with the need to do work and the ability to do work. And he gave people work to do. Christians can use their work to praise God.

Scientists have a special meaning for the word **work**. For scientists, work is done only when energy is transferred to an object so that it moves.

We use force to do work. **Force** is energy such as a push or pull that moves an object.

Place a book on your desk. Use force to push it. Use force to pull it towards you. When the book moves, work is being done. Now push straight down on the book. The desk top keeps the book from moving. Push hard. When the book does not move, no work is being done.

People use machines to make work easier. A **machine** is a device that changes the amount or direction of force. Machines help people do work.

What machines make your work easier?

There are six types of simple machines: the lever, inclined plane, wedge, wheel and axle, and pulley.

work the transfer of energy that causes an object to move

force energy such as a push or pull that moves an object

machine (mə shēn´) a device that changes the amount or direction of force

Is It Work?

pencil
paper

Remember the definition of work? Try some of the following activities and ask if you are transfering energy to an object to make it move.

1. Write your name on the paper. Is it work?
2. Now erase your name. Is it work?
3. Make a fist with both hands. Push them against each other. Is it work?
4. Drop your pencil on the floor. Is it work?
5. Pick up your pencil. Is it work?

Making a Force Measurer

paper fastener   rubber band
heavy cardboard   string
2 paper clips   masking tape

1. Use a paper fastener to attach a rubber band to the top of piece of cardboard that is 5 x 25 cm.
2. Bend two paper clips open. Hook one to the free end of the rubber band.
3. Draw a line on the cardboard at the bottom of the first paper clip. Continue drawing lines, each one centimetter apart, to the bottom of the cardboard.
4. Mark the first line "0." Write "1" on the second line, and so on.
5. Tie loops in both ends of a 15 cm long string. Hook the second paper clip through one of these loops.

You will use your force measurer in the other activities of this chapter.

Focus on the Bible

When God created people, he told them to work. Adam's first job was to name the animals. Adam did not need machines to help him do that work.

God created people with minds that can think and plan and use ideas. People use their minds to invent tools and machines. Genesis 4:19-22 tells about people who made some of the first tools.

Today you depend on machines and tools for many things. Machines help you work and play. They make your clothes, build your houses, and make your toys. Every tool and machine you depend on was invented by a person. But God created people with the minds that made it possible for them to invent machines and tools.

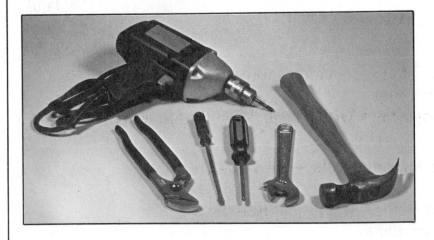

Simple Machines

A **lever** is a simple machine with two arms on either side of a fulcrum (**ful ´ kr əm**). The fulcrum is the point at which a lever turns. The short arm of the lever is placed beneath an object to be lifted. Force is applied to the long arm. When the long arm of the lever moves down, the short arm moves up. The arm raises the object.

lever (**lev ´ ər**) a simple machine with two arms on either side of a fulcrum

A teeter-totter is a lever. When you play on a teeter-totter you push down on one end to lift your partner on the other end. A bottle opener is also a lever. What work does a bottle opener do?

Where Do You Want the Fulcrum?

book
finger
30 cm ruler

Lifting is one way to raise an object. But using a lever makes it easier to raise something.

We will try lifting a book with a lever. What do you think is the best way to do this?

1. Put 1 cm of the ruler under the edge of the book.
2. Use your finger as the fulcrum. Put it under the ruler at the 15 cm mark.
3. Push down on the end of the ruler. Is it very hard to do?
4. Now move the fulcrum (your finger) to the 5 cm mark. Is it easier or harder to move the book?
5. Move the fulcrum to the 25 cm mark. Now is it easier or harder to move the book? How does the placement of the fulcrum make a difference?

An **inclined plane** is a simple machine used to move an object to a higher place. Inclined planes are often called ramps.

Inclined planes can be long or short. Less force is needed to move an object up a long inclined plane than is need to move it up a short inclined plane.

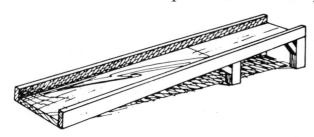

A **screw** is a special kind of inclined plane. A screw is an inclined plane, wrapped in a spiral shape. Cut a piece of paper into a triangle shape. This triangle is like an inclined plane. Wrap it into a tube. Use your finger to trace the edge of the inclined plane as it wraps around the tube. How are screws used?

A **wedge** is a simple machine used to push objects apart.

A knife is a wedge. Axes are wedges that are used to push wood apart. A nail is also a kind of wedge. Name some other wedges.

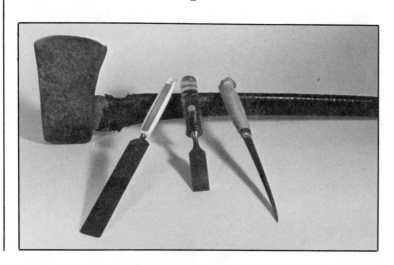

wheel and axle a
simple machine
that has a rod
(axle) on which a
wheel turns

A **wheel and axle** is another simple machine. An axle is the rod on which a wheel turns. Wheels and axles can be used in two ways.

Sometimes force is applied to the wheel. It turns the axle. Door knobs, radio and TV knobs, and steering wheels are examples of this kind of wheel and axle. Less force is needed to turn the large wheel than would be needed to turn the small axle.

Sometimes force is applied to the axle. Then the wheel turns with greater speed. It moves a greater distance than the small axle. When you pedal a bike, your feet move in a small circle, but the wheel moves in a large circle. The bike moves faster than you would if you were walking.

A gear is a special type of wheel and axle. A gear is a wheel with teeth. Gears usually work in pairs. When one gear turns, the other gear also turns.

Measuring Force

force measurer
small weight
several books
string and tape

1. Use several books to make an inclined plane as shown in the drawing.
2. Use string to attach the weight to the force measurer.
3. Pull the weight up the inclined plane. Note how much force (in cm) is needed to move the weight up the inclined plane.
4. Now put the weight back on the table. Lift it up without using the inclined plane. Note the amount of force needed.

How much force did the inclined plane save?

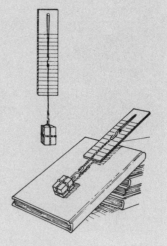

Gears are used to change the speed at which an object turns. A car uses gears to change the speed at which the engine turns the wheels.

When a large gear turns a small gear, more force is needed to turn it. When a small gear turns a large gear, less force is needed.

 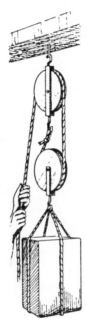

A **pulley** is a simple machine that is a form of the wheel and axle. A pulley is made of a rope and one or more wheels. When a pulley has one wheel, it is used to make work easier by changing the direction of the force. When a pulley has two or more wheels, it makes work easier by lowering the amount of force needed to lift an object.

pulley a simple machine made of a rope and one or more wheels

Focus on Tools

People use tools to build machines. Some tools are themselves simple machines. Tools help make work easier, too. Tools usually do one of seven basic jobs. They are used to measure, cut, shape, drill, hold, fasten, or pound.

Rulers and meter sticks are used to **measure**.
Saws are used to **cut** wood and other materials.
Sanders, files, and planes **shape** wood and other materials.
An electric **drill** makes holes.
Clamps **hold** objects together.
Screws, nails, and bolts **fasten** objects together.
Hammers **pound** objects.

Look at the pictures of these tools. Which tools are simple machines?

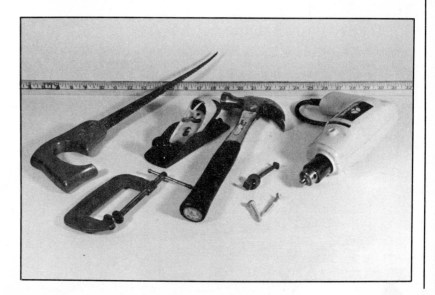

Which Machines?

pencil sharpener

Take a closer look at a common complex machine.

1. Take the cover off of the pencil sharpener. Make sure you have a waste basket underneath it so you don't spill the shavings.
2. What simple machines do you see?
3. Now turn the handle. Do you see any more simple machines?

Complex Machines

Many of the machines that people use have several parts. A machine that is made up of two or more simple machines is called a complex machine.

For example, a scissors is a complex machine. It is made of two wedges and two levers. The levers and wedges work together to cut paper or other objects.

A shovel is another complex machine. It combines a lever and a wedge. The wedge pushes dirt apart. The lever helps lift the dirt. (One of your hands is the fulcrum of the lever.)

A fan is an even more complex machine. It uses electrical energy to move air. A fan has wheels and axles, gears, wedges, and levers.

A car is a complex machine with hundreds of parts. Car shapes are wedges that cut through the air. The steering wheel is a wheel and axle. The brake pedal is a lever. Within the engine are pulleys, gears, levers, and many other parts.

Name some other complex machines. What work do they do?

Technology

People use tools and machines in many ways. **Technology** is the process by which people use tools and energy to change materials into useful objects.

Years ago people used simple technology. They traveled in horse-drawn carts, cooked on wood stoves, and used hand tools.

But technology has grown very rapidly. One hundred years ago people did not have many of the things we take for granted. Cars, television, telephones, air conditioners, washing machines, and other inventions have all come about because of

technology (tek nol´ ə jē) process by which people use tools and energy to change materials into useful objects

technology. Today we can send satellites into space, travel underwater in submarines, or fly in a jet aircraft across the ocean. Some people say we live in an age of technology.

Focus on the Bible

Work is part of God's plan for people. When God created Adam, before sin came into the world, he put Adam into the Garden of Eden and told Adam to "work it and take care of it" (Gen. 2:15).

After Adam and Eve brought sin into the world, work became hard. But work is still part of God's plan for people. He wants us to take care of his creation. That's work. He also wants us to serve him by doing work that helps other people.

Over the years, people have made tools and machines which make work easier. One of the things Christians must think about is how we use tools. As people develop more technology, we must be careful about using it responsibly.

For example, today people use large bulldozers to fill in wetlands like ponds and marshes. When wetlands are filled with dirt, houses can be built on there. People need houses, so it is good that new houses are built. But the plants and animals which lived in the pond community lose their homes when wetlands are filled in. What would happen if all wetlands were filled?

Years ago people used small knives to sharpen pencils. This method was slow, and if you weren't careful with the knife, it was also dangerous. Then someone invented the pencil sharpener. It sharpens pencils quickly and safely. The pencil sharpener makes work easier.

However, pencil sharpeners use up pencils faster. If you put the pencil into the machine and grind the pencil down, you could waste much of the pencil. Wasting pencils uses up trees and graphite.

When we do work the way God wants, we use resources, like those in the pencil, wisely. Think about the ways we can care for forests, for example. Years ago people cut down trees with axes. While the ax is a tool which makes work easier, cutting trees with an ax is still hard work. Because it was hard, people did not cut very many trees. But they often did cut all the trees from an area, leveling the forest.

When power saws and other machines were invented, cutting trees became easier. Today people can cut as many trees as they want. Machines and trucks can carry the trees far from the forest. As a result, many, many more trees are cut today than in years past. Sometimes people still cut all the trees of the forest, but often they only take some of the trees and leave the forest standing. Which method shows more concern for God's creation?

Review

Summary

Work is done when force moves an object. Energy is needed for work. Simple machines include the lever, inclined planes, screw, wedge, wheel and axle, and pulley. Complex machines are made of two or more simple machines working together. God wants people to think about technology and how it affects creation.

Vocabulary

work	wedge
force	inclined plane
machine	wheel and axle
technology	screw
lever	pulley

Review Questions

1. How do machines make work easier?
2. Explain two ways wheels and axles are used.
3. What main kinds of work are tools used for?
4. Give examples of good things technology has brought and problems it has caused.

Chapter 8

Packages

What is a package?
How are packages used?
What do packages tell us about products?

How is your lunch packaged today? Is it in a throw-away bag or in a reusable lunchbox? Look inside your lunch. There may be plastic bags, waxed paper, plastic containers, or other packages in your lunch.

Think about how these packages are used. What job do they do?

A **package** is a wrapper which protects, groups, informs, or beautifies.

package (pak´ ij)
container which protects, groups, informs, or beautifies

Almost everything you and your family buy comes in packages. Food, clothing, tools, and toys come in packages. Often you carry these packages home in another package—a shopping bag. You probably carry your lunch to school in a package, and you might take your homework home in another package—a bookbag.

Try to imagine a world without packages. No bags for flour; no boxes for cereal; no bottles for rootbeer. What would happen in a world without packages?

Packages are made of many materials. Bottles and jars are made of glass. Boxes are usually made of cardboard. Some packages are made of paper. Many packages are made of plastic. Packages can also be made of two or more materials. Cereal packages are made of cardboard with plastic or waxed paper inside. Glass jars often have metal lids.

Try this. Make two lists. In the first list put everything you can think of which does not come in a package. In the second list put things which come in packages. Tell what kind of packages these things usually come in.

Focus on the Bible

People have used packages for a long time. In Bible times, packages helped people protect and move things. Labeling and beautifying were not as important in packaging then.

Look up these Bible verses. Tell what was packaged and how it was packaged.

> Genesis 42:25-28
> 1 Kings 17:12
> Matthew 9:17
> Matthew 26:7
> John 4:27-29

Packages Which Protect

Many packages are designed to protect what is inside. An egg carton is one kind of package which protects. How does an egg carton keep the eggs from breaking?

Here are some other packages which protect the objects or material inside.

- Soft drink bottles protect the soda pop from losing its fizz.
- Cans protect food from spoiling.
- Plastic bags protect clothing from getting dirty.
- Large cardboard boxes protect stoves and refrigerators from scratches.

Name some other packages which protect.

Packages can protect in another way, too. They can protect people from what is inside the package. Nowadays, most medicines are packaged in containers which young children cannot open. Why is this kind of packaging important?

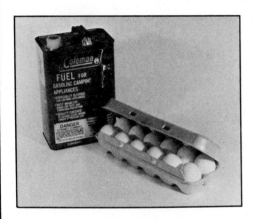

Gasoline is another product that can only be stored in special packages. The government decides which kinds of containers will keep the gas from exploding or burning. Gasoline cans are packages which protect people from injury.

How Many Packages?

How many packages have you seen or used today? Try to make a list of as many as you can remember.

1. Think back before breakfast. Did you brush your teeth? What held the toothpaste?
2. What did you eat for breakfast? What was that food packaged in?
3. What packages are in your desk?
4. What packages did you see your teacher use today?

Using Packages to Group Items

about 30 crayons, pencils, erasers, paperclips
heavy construction paper
scissors, tape, glue

Divide into groups of four or five people.

1. Each group must try to move the same number of items from one side of the room to the other. Follow these rules:

   • You may not use a package.
   • Each person must move the objects part of the way.
   • If anything drops, start over.
   • Time yourselves to see how long it takes.

2. Now design a carrying package for the 20 items. You may want to make a box, an envelope, a tube, or any other kind of package. Your package must hold all the objects.
3. Follow the same rules as before, but this time use the package. How much faster could you move the objects when they were in a package?

Packages Which Group

Many packages group items together. A package which groups items holds many small objects. For example, a cereal box holds hundreds of pieces of cereal. Without a package the cereal would be hard to carry.

Packages can help count items. For example, a big box of crayons holds 64 crayons. It is much easier to buy one box of 64 crayons than it is to count out 64 crayons when you want to buy them.

Most food packages are boxed in larger packages for shipping. For example, a cereal company might send two cases of corn flakes to the grocery store. Each case might contain twelve cartons. Each carton contains hundreds of corn flakes. Without these packages, it would be very hard to buy cereal and to keep it fresh.

Packages Which Beautify

Sometimes packages make the object inside look better. When you wrap presents for birthdays or Christmas, you are making a package which beautifies. Then the person who is getting the present will know it is special.

Companies want you to buy their products. They package their products so you will think they are special. Companies have found that a good-looking package can make shoppers try the product. But they have also found that shoppers will not keep buying a product unless it is a good one, no matter how attractive the package is.

Packages Which Inform

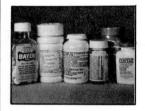

Many packages tell something about the product inside. Most tell how to use the product. Others tell what the product is made of. Still others may warn about dangers from using the product.

Most food products come in packages that tell what is in the food. The packages may tell how to cook it, give ideas about how to serve it, or tell how good it is for you.

Packages may also tell where the product was made, how much it costs, how many pieces are inside, and many other things.

What Is On the Label?

food packages

Study the way that labels give information about the contents of a package.

1. Find 10 food packages. Make a chart like the one shown.
2. Put an **X** on the chart if the information is given on the label.

Product Name	Weight	Ingredients	Nutritional Information	Serving Suggestions	Good Things About Product	Where Made	Bright Pictures	Coupons	Prize Offers

Package Technology

Packaging is big business. Every year, millions and millions of packages are made and used. Package designers are people who work making new packages. First, they make a mock-up. A mock-up is a model package. It shows what a new package will look like.

Some of the new packages designers have invented include plastic squeeze bottles, pop-top cans, and push-botton cans. Designers always try to make packages which are easier to use or which help sell the product.

Several years ago, people bought just enough food for that day. But technology has changed the way we shop. Packages that keep food fresh for a long time make it possible to ship food over long distances. When you go to the grocery store, you can buy things which come from far away. They are in packages which protect them from spoiling. For example, frozen food packages protect foods by keeping them cold. Cans keep food from spoiling for a long time. Packages also protect foods from damage by insects and mice.

Focus on Cans

A few years ago you needed a can opener to open a can of soda pop. Packaging designers wanted to make a can that did not need an opener, so they invented soda pop cans with tabs. You pulled the tab off to open the can.

But the new tabs turned out to be dangerous. Some people swallowed the tabs by accident. A few people died. The tabs were also sharp, and people sometimes cut themselves on the new tabs.

So designers invented another kind of opener. They invented pop-top cans. These new cans had a tab which did not come off. The opening just pushed into the can. These new cans were safer. Today, when you buy a can of soda pop, it probably comes with a pop top.

Stewardship

Packages are useful. Without packages, your life would be harder. Buying and carrying products would be hard. But packages also cause problems. Most packages are throw-away packages. After the product has been used, we throw the package away. You and your family probably throw away about 1000 kg of used packages every year. (That's more than a ton!)

Paper, cardboard, and most plastic packages are thrown away after they are used.

Make a list of some of the packages you throw away every day.

What happens to the packages you throw away? Most garbage is picked up by garbage trucks. They carry the used packages and other garbage to a dump or landfill. Every year, people throw away mountains of packages and other garbage. Plastic packages, paper and cardboard packages, metal packages, and glass packages are all dumped into landfills.

When packages are wasted, several problems happen.

First, resources are used up. Plastics are made from oil. Oil is a non-renewable resource. That means when people use up all the oil in the world, there will be no more. When plastics are thrown away, the oil resources used to make the plastics are wasted.

Paper and cardboard are made from wood. When paper and cardboard packages are thrown away, the wood is wasted. New trees must be cut to make new paper packaging.

Another major problem which results from throwing away packages is that we are running out of places to put garbage. When landfills are full, new places must be turned into dumps. More and more places are turned into landfills every year.

Plastic does not decompose. The decomposers which turn dead plants, food, and paper into basic materials cannot eat plastic. When plastic is thrown away, it remains in the earth. God's natural recycling system does not recycle plastic.

stewardship (stoo´ ərd ship) the care of God's world

Stewardship is taking care of God's creation. How Christians use packaging is part of their stewardship. Soft drinks can be bought in cans or bottles which are thrown away or they can be bought in cans and bottles which are used over. If bottles and cans are thrown away, new packages must be made from fresh resources. The old cans and bottles fill up a dump.

You can carry your lunch to school in a paper bag which you throw away, or you can use a lunch box over and over. Which method of packaging your lunch is less wasteful?

What happens to grocery bags after you bring them home from the store? How many ways are there to use grocery bags over again?

Reusing packages is one way to show stewardship. Christian stewardship can also affect how you buy packages. Some products are packaged wastefully. Can you think of some examples of wasteful packaging.

Stewardship also encourages recycling. Many products can be used again in one form or another. Newspapers can be ground up to make pulp for new paper. Some glass bottles can be refilled and used again. Some plastics can be melted down to use for other products. Does your community have a recycling program? How could you and your class participate?

Review

Summary

Almost every product you buy is packaged in some way. Packages protect products and people. They are also used to group, beautify, and inform. Many packages are thrown away after they are used. You can make choices about how you use packaging.

Vocabulary

package   stewardship

Review Questions

1. How would life be different without packages?
2. Why do companies package products in beautiful packages?
3. How can Christians use packages in a way which shows stewardship?

Supplementary Material

Measuring Temperature

Most people in the world use the **Celsius** scale to measure temperature.

Temperature is measured in degrees on the Celsius scale. The symbol for degrees is °.

Water freezes at 0° Celsius. It boils at 100°. Average human body temperature is 37°.

The bulb at the bottom of a thermometer is sensitive to temperature changes. When the temperature around the bulb changes, the red alcohol inside becomes larger or smaller. The change can be read on the scale along the side of the glass tube.

Celsius (sel ´ se əs) measure of temperature; abbreviation: C

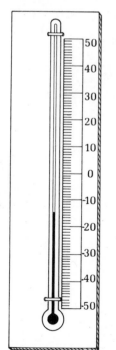

A cold day in January

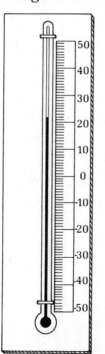

Common room temperature

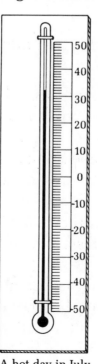

A hot day in July

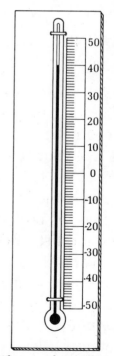

When you have a fever

133

Practice Measuring Temperature

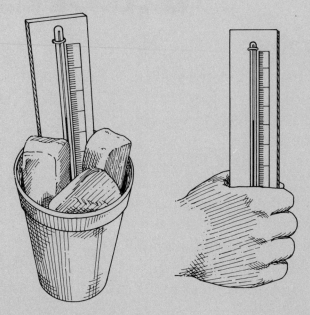

thermometer
crushed ice (or ice cubes)
paper or plastic cup

WARNING: Use alcohol, not mercury, thermometers. (Alcohol is red, mercury is silver.)

1. When measuring temperature, leave the thermometer in place for 3 or 4 minutes before reading it.
2. Place your thermometer in a cup of ice. Wait. Read the temperature on the thermometer. How cold is the ice?
3. Hold the bulb of the thermometer in your closed fist. Wait at least 4 minutes. How warm is your hand?
4. Measure several other temperatures. Try the air temperature near the classroom heater, near a window, outdoors, in the hallway or gym, or other places.

Data Charts

Observing closely can help you identify change. Data charts can help you communicate change. One kind of data chart is a **histogram**. A histogram is a chart that shows how many.

Like other charts, a histogram organizes information (data) in a way that is easy to read. In a histogram, bars are drawn to show number. The longer the bar, the larger the number.

To read a histogram, look at the end of the bar. The number of the line at the bar's end is the number for that bar.

Histograms can communicate information about many things. Remember they always tell how many.

Study these histograms. What does each one tell you?

GRADE FOUR PETS

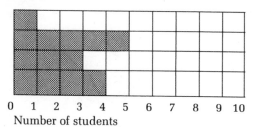

GRADE FOUR SHOE COLOR

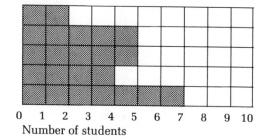

Another type of data chart that shows change is a line graph. A **line graph** shows changes over time. Things that change slowly are often described by a line graph.

In a line graph, points are made to show how a thing is changing. The points are connected with a line.

Look at the line graph and pictures below. The line graph shows how the plant is growing each day. How tall was the plant on the second day? How tall was it on the fifth day?

PLANT GROWTH

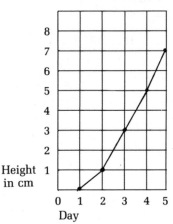

Practice Making Charts

Histograms

1. Copy this chart onto your paper.
2. List these hair colors on the chalkboard. Count how many people in the class have each hair color. Write the number beside the color.
3. Fill in the histogram to show *how many* students have each color.

GRADE FOUR HAIR COLOR

Brown
Black
Blonde
Red

0 1 2 3 4 5 6 7 8 9 10
Number of students

Line Graphs

1. Copy this chart onto your paper.

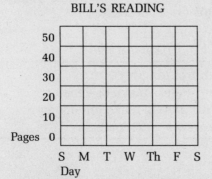

BILL'S READING

2. Study the information below. It shows how many pages of a book Bill read each day.

	Sunday:	12 pages
	Monday:	20 pages
	Tuesday:	32 pages
	Wednesday:	17 pages
	Thursday:	15 pages
	Friday:	25 pages
	Saturday:	3 pages

3. Draw a point on the graph for each day's reading. Put it where the line for the day and the line for the number of pages cross.

4. Use a ruler to draw straight lines between the points.

CHART OF METRIC UNITS OF MEASURE

All spellings and abbreviations are American.
Canadian spellings and abbreviations are in brackets [ ].

LENGTH

Unit	Abbreviation	Definition
meter [metre]	m	basic unit of length
centimeter [centimetre]	cm	100 centimeters make one meter
millimeter [millimetre]	mm	1000 millimeters make one meter
kilometer [kilometre]	km	1 kilometer is 1000 meters

VOLUME

Unit	Abbreviation	Definition
liter [litre]	l [L]	basic unit of volume
milliliter [millilitre]	ml [mL]	1000 milliliters make one liter

TEMPERATURE

Unit	Abbreviation	Definition
Celsius	C	scale for measuring temperature
degree	$^\circ$	units on the Celsius scale

-10° C	a cold winter day
0° C	water freezes
20° C	room temperature
30° C	hot summer day
37° C	human body temperature
100° C	water boils

Glossary

air mass a large body of air

atmosphere (**at**´ mə sfîr) the layer of air around the earth

blade (blād) the broad, flattened part of a leaf

cartilage (**kär** tl ij) tough tissue that connects bones

Celsius (**sel**´ sē əs) measure of temperature; abbreviation: **C**

cirrus (**sir**´ əs) high, feathery clouds

classify (**klas**´ ə fī) sort into groups by characteristics

community (kə **myoo**´ ni tē) the groups of organisms living in a
   specific area

condensation (kon´ den **sā**´ shən) the process of tiny particles in the
   air joining to form water droplets

continental shelf (kon´ tə **nen**´ tl shelf) the slanting area beyond the
   shore

cumulus (**kyoo**´ myə ləs) billowy white clouds

evaporation (i **vap**´ ə rā shən) the change of water into vapor in the
   air

force energy such as a push or pull that moves an object

frequency (**frē**´ kwən sē) speed of vibration

front the leading edge of an air mass

fungus (**fung**´ gəs) plants which do not make their own food

habitat (**hab**´ i tat) area in which an organism normally lives

high pressure condition in which particles are closer together in cool
   air

histogram (**his**´ tə gram) a chart that shows how many

humidity (hyoo **mid**´ i tē) the amount of water in the air

inclined plane (in **klīnd**´ plān) a simple machine used to move
   objects to a higher place

joint a point where two bones are joined

kelp large brown seaweed

larva (**lär**´ və) a young insect which does not look like the adult

lever (lĕv´ ər) a simple machine with two arms on either side of a fulcrum

ligament (lig´ ə mənt) tough, stretchy tissue which connects bones

line graph a data chart that shows change over time

low pressure condition in which particles are farther apart in warm air

machine (mə shēn´) a device that changes the amount or direction of force

marrow (mar´ ō) soft material in bones, consisting of fat cells, blood cells, and tissue

noise (noiz) unwanted, unpleasant, or unexpected sound

nutrients (nōō´ trē ənts) ingredients that help build up the body

nymph (nimf) a young insect which looks like the adult

ocean (ō´ shən) the mass of salt water that covers the earth

organism (ôr´ gə niz əm) any living thing

package (pak´ ij) container which protects, groups, informs, or beautifies

petiole (pet´ ē ōl) stalk that attaches a leaf to the stem

pitch (pich) the quality of a sound that makes it seem high or low

plankton (plangk´ tən) tiny plants and animals which live in the ocean

precipitation (pri sip´ i tā´ shən) the process of water droplets falling from the clouds to earth

process (pros´ es) to prepare, treat, or change food

pulley a simple machine made of a rope and one or more wheels

resonance (rez´ ə nəns) reinforcement of sound by vibration in a second object

screw an inclined plane cut in a spiral

skeleton (skel´ i tən) a framework of bones

sound a form of energy you can hear

stewardship (stōō´ ərd ship) the care of God's world

stratus (strā´ təs) clouds that hang in low, flat sheets

succession (sək sesh´ ən) orderly changes in a habitat

technology (tek nol´ ə jē) process by which people use tools and energy to change materials into useful objects

tendon (ten dən) cord which connects muscles to bones

vibration (vi **brā**´ shən) rapid back and forth movement

wedge a simple machine used to push objects apart

wheel and axle a simple machine that has a rod (axle) on which a wheel turns

work the transfer of energy that causes an object to move